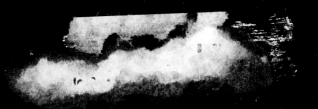

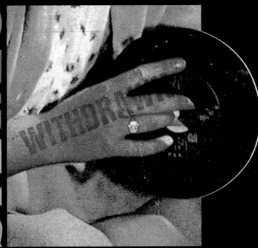

STEREO

WITHDRAWN

D0331095

ROCK AROUND·THE

Don & Eddie

CLOCK

Fire Colleg

Don't Kn

ck The Rock

UCTION · A COLUMBIA PICTURE

THE KING OF
ROCK 'N' ROLL!

**ALAN
FREED**

IN

ROCK,
ROCK,
ROCK

Don't Kn

A CL

ck The Rock

UCTION · A COLUMBIA PICTURE

CONTENTS

THE STORY OF ROCK
SMASH HITS AND SUPERSTARS

Alain Dister

THAMES AND HUDSON

The year was 1945. The Second World War had just ended in a flash over Hiroshima. The GIs came back home longing for peace and domestic happiness, but found that the old values were dying. And the music was changing – young people were rejecting the old-fashioned sounds of the conservative white adult world and turning to the fresh and witty voices of certain black singers.

CHAPTER 1

THE PIONEERS

Black rhythm and blues seduced young white music lovers with its raw energy. Its heir, rock and roll, produced a similar passion, though the songs of Bill Haley (opposite), for example, could not claim the vitality of their models.

1954. General Dwight David Eisenhower was president. Ten years earlier his GIs and British forces had made history on the beaches of Normandy and across Europe. Ever since, the United States had been the international symbol of rediscovered liberty and happiness.

Yet the Cold War was in full swing, stirred up by the seemingly permanent threat of nuclear conflict with the USSR. The fear of Communism incited a witch-hunt led by Senator Joseph McCarthy, and intellectuals were his first victims. But this repressive atmosphere did not impede the strong artistic current flowing between New York and San Francisco. It was the time of beatniks, of (to use the Beat terms) desolation angels and celestial bums, rebels, and lovers of jazz, poetry and the road. They even looked alike: writers Jack Kerouac and his friend Neal Cassady, actors James Dean and Marlon Brando, and artists Jackson Pollock and Robert Frank. They wore T-shirts, blue jeans and leather jackets, and had cool looks, guarded gazes and provocative smiles – all fragile, crazy and free.

In the mid-fifties James Dean (above left) and Marlon Brando (above) personified the rebellious teenager.

America in black and white

Behind Kerouac's literary road and the photographic path taken by Frank loomed a country that was a victim of its own emptiness and immobility, no longer looking forward to anything, without future, without hope. The pursuit of happiness guaranteed by the Constitution found its realization in a consumer frenzy and a petty regulated existence in which 'dangerous' – or 'immoral' – activities such as sexual relations, motorcycle rides and certain types of dancing were prohibited. Middle-class white society

Neal Cassady (below left) was the model for the hero of *On the Road*, the novel-manifesto of the Beat Generation written by his friend Jack Kerouac (below right).

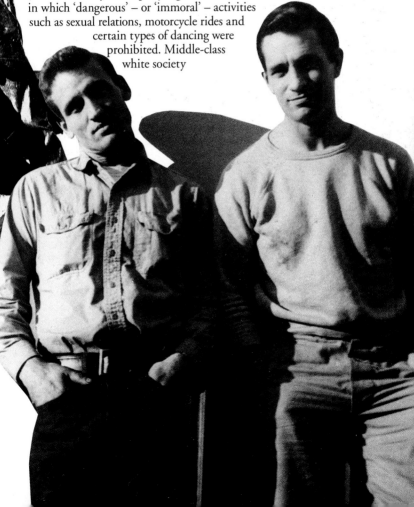

prospered, resigned, self-satisfied and suspicious of its neighbours – particularly its black neighbours.

One hundred years after the end of the Civil War, blacks did not enjoy their full civil rights. Southern states still practised segregation, and most blacks' economic level, urban as well as rural, was extremely low. Set apart culturally from the white community, blacks invented their own forms of expression, particularly in the musical field, and created systems of independent distribution for it: record labels, concert circuits, local radio stations. Simply by listening to those stations, white teenagers discovered, to their great relief, music far more lively than the tunes being sung by Bing Crosby and Frank Sinatra, the stars of the day.

Blacks invent a new dance – rock and roll

Everything began with, on the one hand, jazz and blues – especially 'boogie-woogie' blues piano – and, on the other, gospel. The first kind of music was played in the bars, 'juke joints', and dance halls; the second was sung in churches. In fact, some of the biggest rock and rhythm and blues artists made their debuts accompanied by small, out-of-tune organs, behind a preacher. Vocal groups like the Ink Spots, which were very popular in the thirties, were also descended from gospel. One music would devote itself to the secular virtues of teenage romance, and the other would remain deeply religious.

Blues singers occasionally found more lucrative outlets in bands that played on the weekends for social occasions. One popular dance, developed in the forties, was named 'rock and roll'. To balance, to roll, to reel, to spin ... the graphic vocabulary of the black world had little in common with repressed white ways when it came to describing physical or sexual pleasure. Often backed by a honking saxophone, certain singers known as 'shouters' had begun to emphasize the beat by screaming, a technique inherited directly from preachers. Little Richard, Screamin' Jay Hawkins and, to a lesser extent, Ray Charles, exemplify this style.

A pianist, organist, saxophonist and – primarily – a singer, much inspired by gospel music, Ray Charles

At the beginning of the fifties, teenagers were unhappy with the world being offered them and turned to popular black rhythms to help them reinvent a style, a music, an attitude.
Right: Ray Charles, the great voice of gospel-flavoured blues.

skilfully combined the best of blues, jazz and soul. Discovered by Atlantic Records producer Jerry Wexler, Ray Charles recorded several tunes in the fifties that were immediately popular with young audiences: 'I Got a Woman', 'What'd I Say' and 'Hit the Road, Jack'. Strongly influenced by rhythm and blues, this

was rock and roll music before the term was even defined.

Fats Domino

Enormously exciting for the teenagers who discovered it, this music was often recorded in makeshift studios in Memphis, St Louis and Chicago, on the old migration path to the north, marking these cities as capitals of the blues. Black radio stations in the south were the first to broadcast it, well before big cities like New York or Los Angeles. Small labels (Vee Jay, Ace, King) flourished, featuring stars like Howlin' Wolf – who recorded in Memphis with producer Sam Phillips – Muddy Waters and Sonny Boy Williamson. They were

The first bands of pianist Fats Domino (below) were already playing rock and roll at the end of the forties.

RATTLE AND ROCK!

The children of white puritan society derived a certain pleasure in singing lyrics with suggestive innuendos. 'Shake', 'rattle', 'rock' and 'roll' evoked, in a roundabout way, amorous passion and physical release. Black musicians commonly used such jubilant expressions. Their white imitators, like Bill Haley, toned down the meanings to shield themselves from censure and to increase record sales.

great musicians, experienced bluesmen who charged up the old blues idiom with electricity.

At the same time further south, in New Orleans, pianists ruled, playing a musical style born in the brothels and barrelhouses of the French Quarter. Dave Bartholomew ('The Monkey') and Fats Domino ('Blueberry Hill', 'My Blue Heaven', 'Ain't That a Shame') played music that combined the influences of boogie-woogie, traditional jazz inherited from Jelly Roll Morton and Fats Waller, and the energetic rhythm and blues of dance halls. They enjoyed a solid local reputation well before the historic appearance of rock and roll.

The exact date of the birth of rock and roll is difficult to determine

Was rock and roll born in late 1951, when the irrepressible and melodramatic singer Johnnie Ray imitated dance-hall shouters? Or in July 1954, when a shy young man, Elvis Presley, is said to have knocked on the door of Sam Phillips' studio with the idea of cutting a record for his mother's birthday? Or in

Johnnie Ray (below) invented a very personal style. In the course of his concerts, he cried, begged, choked and went into contortions. Many early rockers modelled themselves on him.

March 1955, when the film *Blackboard Jungle* made Bill Haley's 'Rock Around the Clock' a smash hit? Or, that same year, when disc jockey and promoter Alan Freed claimed to baptize the new fashionable dance with the name 'rock 'n' roll'?

The date matters little. This music, in one form or another, had existed for a long time. What changed is that certain show-business tycoons calculated that if rock and roll remained exclusively black property, blacks would receive all the profits – and the profits would necessarily be limited. It seemed critical to open rock up to the huge white market. But the moguls needed an acceptable product – what white teenager could identify with the potentially off-putting image of a Howlin' Wolf or a Sonny Boy Williamson? The new image of rock and roll would be one decked out with all the appropriate enticements of youth, beauty and rebelliousness. James Dean in *Rebel Without a Cause* and Marlon Brando in *The Wild One*

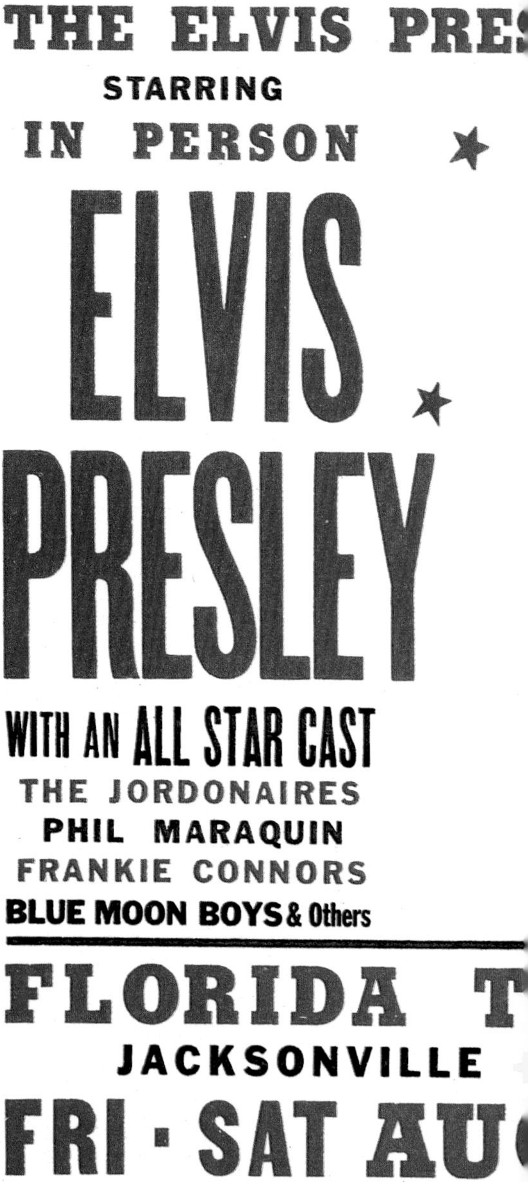

THE ELVIS PRES

STARRING

IN PERSON ★

ELVIS

PRESLEY

WITH AN ALL STAR CAST
THE JORDONAIRES
PHIL MARAQUIN
FRANKIE CONNORS
BLUE MOON BOYS & Others

FLORIDA T

JACKSONVILLE

FRI · SAT AU

Y SHOW had already shown the way. They embodied this vague feeling of defiance against an adult world perceived as a generator of boredom, submission and cowardice.

'If I could find a white man who had the negro sound and the negro feel, I could make a billion dollars' – Sam Phillips

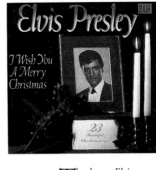

Elvis Presley grabbed the opportunity. A truck driver with slightly too-long hair, flashy clothing and a crooked half-smile, he looked like a rebel. The exterior seemed hard, but the heart was tender. He loved his parents, his mother especially, and visited churches more often than bars. His only fault, in the eyes of staunch southern traditionalists, would be his interest in black music.

The devout Elvis practised by singing hymns and accompanying himself on the organ at home.

Once he became famous Elvis was always accompanied by professional guitarists and held a guitar only when posing for the camera. Overleaf: Elvis in concert, 1956. Pages 24–5: from *Loving You*, 1957.

Elvis Aron (later changed to Aaron) Presley, born
in 1935 in Mississippi, was familiar with B. B. King,
Howlin' Wolf, Arthur 'Big Boy' Crudup and all the
other great blues performers, and he set about to sing
like them, imitating their inflections, their accents, their
guttural style. There was and there will always be two
Elvises: the nice boy – good to his mother, quiet, a
devout Christian, a lover of gospel – and the rocker with
the sensual pout, ready to surrender to every excess. He
was a perfect image of the Deep South, torn between his
religious feelings and his violent urges, his love of God
and his appetite for pleasure. The 'good' Elvis went to
record a love song for his mother. The 'wild' Elvis cut
loose between takes and bawled out a well-known rock
and roll song.

The latter is evidently what attracted the attention
of producer Sam Phillips, head of Sun Records. Phillips
had learned that increasing numbers of young whites
were buying blues and rhythm and blues records. With
Elvis he believed he had finally found that rare creature,
a white man who sang like he was black, thus creating
an infinitely larger commercial potential. In July 1954
he recorded Elvis singing 'That's All Right', a popular
tune by Arthur Crudup (who would never see much
of the money the song brought in). Elvis was supported
by studio musicians Scotty Moore (guitar) and Bill Black
(bass). These 'good old boys' from Tennessee were more
used to playing country music but did not mind the
rougher idiom of rhythm and blues. This approach
of putting muscles on country music was dubbed
'rockabilly'. Elvis' first and best recordings ('Good
Rockin' Tonight', 'Milkcow Blues Boogie' and
'Mystery Train') attest to this clever combination
of black music and cowboy serenades.

Jerry Lee Lewis, the killer

With Elvis Presley's first record in black and white –
one side black music, the other country – Sun Records
broke a music industry rule: the racial unity of artistic
productions. With the introduction of Jerry Lee
Lewis on the same label, it broke a second: the
avoidance of explicit lyrics. Lewis appropriated

the raw language of black blues singers who were not shy about using metaphors to express passion ('Great Balls of Fire').

Lewis had attended fundamentalist Bible schools before selling his soul to the devil. A remarkable pianist, he had appeared on stage since adolescence, touring markets and fairs with his father; their piano was installed on the back of a flatbed truck. Jerry Lee played a vigorous boogie-woogie. Offstage, the young man tasted the pleasures of the road – alcohol, gambling, women.

The Lewis family was constantly split between religious exaltation and debauchery. Lewis' cousin, the famous televangelist Jimmy Swaggart, is as celebrated for his fiery sermons as for losing his way in the shady sections of town. In the Lewises' congregation, the Pentecostal Assembly of God Church (which Elvis also attended), the parishioners sang until they fell into a trance. They spoke in tongues and beat themselves, while confessing to all sorts of base acts, particularly sexual ones. And no sooner did they leave the church than they resumed their old habits – the trips to go-go bars, the binges and the poker parties: 'Whole Lotta Shakin' Goin' On'.

White country and western music meets black blues

The craziness of rock and roll life, however, did not infect all of its performers. Compared to the escapades of a Jerry Lee Lewis or a Little Richard, the life of a Carl Perkins or a Bill Haley seems very settled. Perkins was part of the Sun stable before Lewis arrived. A down-to-earth country musician, Perkins had no problem slightly modifying the rhythm of his music to write more rock and roll–type songs like 'Blue Suede Shoes'. He joined Elvis – who borrowed the song from him and made it a hit – and Jerry Lee Lewis as one of the premier early rock and rollers.

Like other musicians of this

Little Richard (below) was torn between the church and the street.

generation, Perkins followed the
path traced by Hank Williams,
a true legend of country music.
Hank Williams' music, with its blues
strains, captured the spirit – if not
the letter – of rock and roll and broke
with the canons of traditional country
music. While Williams was declared *persona
non grata* at the staid
Grand Ole Opry in
Nashville, those up
north in the big cities paid
little attention to a controversy
engendered by what they
perceived as some
backward country folk
clinging to the old ideas of
racial segregation. And, in
any case, they preferred
Bill Haley and His
Comets.

'Rock Around the Clock'

From the
beginning
of the
fifties,
Bill Haley,
a former disc
jockey, blended
rhythm and blues hits
into his repertoire of
country and western classics.
Inevitably, the new sounds
met with a favourable response
from young audiences,
even though – to satisfy the
morality guidelines established
by a puritanical white society –
he sanitized the contents of
some of his songs; somewhat
obscene in Joe Turner's original

BILL HALEY AND HIS COMETS

The acrobatic
contortions of rock
and roll dances were
descended from black
dances like the boogie-
woogie, the black bottom
and the shimmy. This
physical abandon did
little to enhance the
reputation of rock in
traditionalists' minds.

version, 'Shake, Rattle and Roll' was transformed by Bill Haley into an innocuous teenage ditty. But the rhythm remained, and the term 'rock' soon found itself associated with a series of songs that spread the new musical message far and wide.

THE NEWEST BIGGEST ROCK'N'ROLL MOVIE OF ALL!

In 1955 movies were passionate about the new phenomenon of rock and roll and spread images of its creators around the world.

ALAN FREED

LITTLE RICHARD

DAVE APPELL AND HIS APPLEJACKS

Bill Haley (above) and promoter Alan Freed are often credited with the invention of the term 'rock 'n' roll'.

The famous 'Rock Around the Clock', recorded in April 1954, holds a key position in the story of this music. The song's importance would be measured the next year, when it appeared on the soundtrack of the newly released film *Blackboard Jungle*. Thus began a strange life for Bill Haley and His Comets. These chubby, overgrown teenagers, these easy-going nice guys who set upon black rhythms, found themselves speaking for rebellious youth. Their concerts turned into riots; their names appeared on the leather jackets of rebels the world over.

If rock music aroused such passion on its own, what would happen when its performers also adopted the image of potentially dangerous rebels?

Wild escapades

Despite his appearance and his posturing on stage, Elvis didn't scare anyone. He had become 'acceptable' since his signing with RCA, where, under the control of his manager 'Colonel' Tom Parker, he recorded dreamy ballads ('Love Me Tender', 'Crying In the Chapel'). But Gene Vincent, Eddie Cochran and, a little later, Vince Taylor were more threatening. These tough guys were worthy heirs to Brando's motorcycle gangs and lived up to rock and roll's

Eddie Cochran (below) shortly before his death in a car accident in 1960.

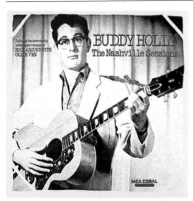

reputation for excess and violence propagated by the media. In black leather from head to toe, they presented a frightening image to parents. Gene Vincent ('Be-Bop-a-Lula') and Eddie Cochran ('Summertime Blues') recharged the dissident spirit of rock and roll. Their style, their image and even their clothes became an inspiration for many young Americans.

Although his appearance as a bespectacled student was more reassuring, Buddy Holly was not any less of a rebel. He turned his back on traditional country music, adding percussion and a beat borrowed from rhythm and blues. With his band, the Crickets, Buddy the Texan gave his seal of approval to rockabilly. His great hits, both in 1957, 'That'll Be the Day' and 'Peggy Sue', heralded a prolific career, but Holly died tragically at twenty-eight on 3 February 1959 in a plane crash that also took the life of singer Ritchie Valens, the youthful composer of 'La Bamba'.

When Buddy Holly (left) died in 1959, rock lost one of its most prolific composers.

Gene Vincent and His Blue Caps (below). The rockabilly 'bad boy' was the last rebel of the golden age of the pioneers.

The year was 1955. Parents were dismayed by their children's new look, which featured slicked-back hair like James Dean's and Elvis Presley's. Teenagers smoked, dressed in blue jeans and leather jackets, and were swept away by the new dances. They flirted and drove convertibles. The strong wind of change, imagination, rebellion and freedom started in the United States and then blew over the whole western world.

CHAPTER 2

THE INVENTION OF THE TEENAGER

Teenagers led the way at the dawn of the fifties. Young Americans wanted to be free. Rock and roll replaced jazz and country music on the jukebox. The record industry had discovered the teenage world.

In 1955 teenagers had economic power, often accompanied by a consumer frenzy equal to that of their parents. They created a new market, which from that time on was flooded with products made especially for their consumption: brand-name leather jackets and the Brando T-shirt, the Thunderbird and the Corvette of the Hollywood playboys, films and Marvel comics. And, of course, records. The 45 rpm single had just made its appearance, and the portable record player allowed teenagers to take over the

The first rock and roll singers left their imprint on street style. Teenagers sported Eddie Cochran hairstyles, Buddy Holly jackets and Carl Perkins blue suede shoes.

world of sound. Until then, to play music they had been dependent on the good mood of their fathers, who were usually in charge of the cumbersome record player enthroned in the family room.

In those carefree and economically developing times, the media, sociologists and parents suddenly discovered a new phenomenon: the teenager.

The new rock and roll hits gradually replaced the old standards. Thanks to the jukebox, rock could be heard in all the teenage hangouts.

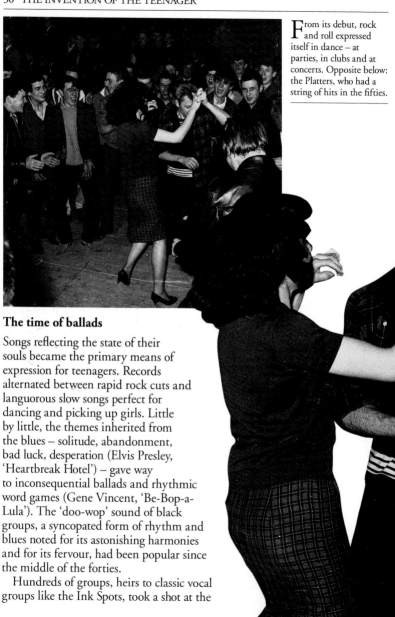

The time of ballads

Songs reflecting the state of their souls became the primary means of expression for teenagers. Records alternated between rapid rock cuts and languorous slow songs perfect for dancing and picking up girls. Little by little, the themes inherited from the blues – solitude, abandonment, bad luck, desperation (Elvis Presley, 'Heartbreak Hotel') – gave way to inconsequential ballads and rhythmic word games (Gene Vincent, 'Be-Bop-a-Lula'). The 'doo-wop' sound of black groups, a syncopated form of rhythm and blues noted for its astonishing harmonies and for its fervour, had been popular since the middle of the forties.

Hundreds of groups, heirs to classic vocal groups like the Ink Spots, took a shot at the

hit parade. The best known remain the
Coasters ('Yakety Yak'), the Drifters
('On Broadway'), the Five Satins ('In
the Still of the Night'), the Moonglows,
the Penguins, the Cadillacs, the Olympics,
the Flamingos and, above all, the Platters
with their long series of hit songs ('Only
You', 'The Great Pretender', 'Smoke Gets
in Your Eyes').

Groups of lyricists and composers
wrote ballads especially for the teenage
market. Songwriting teams like Mort
Shuman/Doc Pomus, Jerry Leiber/Mike
Stoller, and Gerry Goffin/Carole King
were famous for writing a number of
small masterpieces of adolescent
romance, all marked by false hope,
flowery poetry and a penchant
for silliness. Some texts
verged on the absurd,

like 'Surfin' Bird', based on the Rivingtons' songs but performed by the Trashmen. Twenty years later some bands in the New York punk rock scene would be inspired by this stripped-down rock and roll.

Chuck Berry: duck walks and guitar riffs

The development of local radio stations and the rapid growth in the record market conferred on disc jockeys an increasingly important place in the structure of the music business; they now had the power of life and death over an artist's work. Some were tempted by contractual agreements that paid them large sums of money in exchange for repeatedly broadcasting certain songs.
Promoter and DJ

Heir to a long, popular tradition, Chuck Berry's stage show was very suggestive. His famous 'duck walk' (left) was adopted later by admiring white musicians like Keith Richards.

Alan Freed, for example, realizing the potential of young composer-lyricist Chuck Berry, insisted that the musician share with him the profits of his first songs. In exchange, Freed played and promoted them on the air, and in this manner 'Maybellene' reached the hit parade in 1955.

This song, like the majority of those written by Berry, dealt

More than the movies of the time, rock and roll reflected the desire of a generation striving to free itself from all prohibitions – especially those regarding sex. After childhood, but before adulthood, adolescence was that difficult in-between age.

N-BETWEEN AGE

with an aspect of the adolescent world – in this case, the car. Others evoked school ('School Day'), hanging out on Saturday night ('No Particular Place to Go') and feelings about growing up ('Almost Grown'). Many of the lyrics could be read as social commentaries on the era, written with the verve and the sly, innuendo-filled humour of a blues singer well acquainted with the world.

Fascinated by Muddy Waters, Berry had no trouble slightly modifying the blues sound to fashion what would

pajama party

become the definitive rock and roll rhythm. His varied stage performances – featuring his famous duck walk – allowed him to escape stylistic traps such as the ones that caught his colleague Bo Diddley. Berry would remain famous for his series of guitar riffs repeated in tune after tune, and his rhythmic energy was widely imitated.

Rock and roll was immensely popular at the end of the fifties

Rock and roll, a mélange of gospel, rhythm and blues, and country and western, broke into multiple categories. There was a world of difference between, for example, the sweet Paul Anka and a sinning pastor like Little Richard. Paul Anka personified a generation of new rock and roll stars. Even with the phenomenal success of songs like 'Diana', he gave the impression of a being a nice guy – inoffensive, reassuring and respectable – as did those 'sweet-faced' early rockers like Ricky Nelson ('Hello Mary Lou') and the Everly Brothers ('Wake Up Little Susie'). The Everlys revived a vocal style based on rich harmonies that had been popular in the thirties and forties. Their lessons were learned by other groups, as would be seen a short time later with the Beach Boys and the Beatles.

Little Richard (Richard Wayne Penniman) – who was homosexual – had an entirely different image. He furiously played pure rock and roll piano, complete with moves as acrobatic as Jerry Lee Lewis'. But occasional work as a preacher showed through in such spirited compositions as 'Lucille' and 'Long Tall Sally'. Little Richard perfectly embodied two poles of rock.

Disaster

Towards the end of the fifties, rock and roll seemed to have lost its initial vitality. Its founding fathers had all been struck down by fate – often with a helping hand from the Establishment. In the most shocking case of all, Little Richard, the man who summed up the

A well-bred, late-fifties copy of Elvis Presley, Ricky Nelson (below) wrote several memorable songs like 'Hello Mary Lou'.

THE ROCK'N'ROLL RE-ISSUE SERIES.
RICKY

Little Richard (right) proclaimed himself 'the king of rock and roll', like Elvis Presley. A jealous guardian of his title, he forbade his companions to dress like him. In 1965 Jimi Hendrix was dismissed from the band for forgetting the rules. Thoroughly eccentric, Little Richard abandoned music in 1957 to dedicate himself to selling Bibles. He would later return to the stage, however, with his extravagant personality still intact.

philosophy of rock with the immortal phrase 'A-wop-bop-aloo-bop-a-lop-bam-boom', abandoned rock and roll temporarily in 1957 to become Pastor Penniman.

The year 1958 began with Elvis Presley's departure for the army. 'Colonel' Tom Parker had finally tamed the King's rebellious image, and from this point on Elvis had to behave like the rest of the world – to reassure America and, at the same time, to enhance his commercial potential. If Elvis was not totally lost to rock (he still sang pretty ballads), the myth he incarnated was definitely over.

STEINWAY & SONS

A. HANLEY

From now on, he would be – for the media, at least –
a good family man, married to the daughter of his army
colonel and working ardently under the direction of his
manager. What did it matter if the work in question
consisted of an uninterrupted series of worthless films?

This year also saw the premature end of Jerry Lee
Lewis' career. To start with, his marriage to his thirteen-
year-old cousin Myra did not endear the media to him.
During a successful tour in Britain, he was brought down
with arrows shot by the British press. From that time on
he would have to content himself with playing country
music, only occasionally showing feeble flashes
of his old brilliance.

The revenge of Uncle Sam

The next year, 1959, was even more catastrophic. This
was the year of Buddy Holly's plane accident; it also
marked Chuck Berry's descent into hell. Puritan America
had had its eye on Berry for a while –
a black man at the top of the hit
parade! And one who spoke to
teenagers so suggestively! The
opportunity to corner him
presented itself when he broke a
federal law prohibiting the crossing
of a state line in the company of a

minor. He claimed that nothing had happened, that the girl had lied about her age and that his trial was rigged for racist reasons, but, finally, at the end of a long trial and an appeal, he was sentenced to three years in prison. He served two years. The early success of the Beatles and the Rolling Stones can be seen as tributes to his work and helped rehabilitate him in the eyes of the public.

In 1960 fate dealt a blow to still more pioneers of rock. The taxi taking Eddie Cochran and Gene Vincent from a concert at the end of a British tour crashed. Cochran was killed instantly, while Vincent recovered from serious injuries.

Middle America relaxed; it could now return to the old values. Already, in small towns people burned records and hung posters calling for boycotts of stations broadcasting the music that had launched the rock and roll movement.

All those who had stood as indomitable rebels were now either toeing the line or dead. The Establishment could only offer antiseptic singers – like Frankie Avalon, Bobby Rydell and Fabian – respectable, pale imitations of rockers, standard show-business products focusing on the most inoffensive teenage themes. For the time being the torrid lyrics inherited from the tradition of the blues gave way to shallow ditties.

However, rock had left its imprint on the subconscious of an entire generation. With its raw energy, its coolness and its openness, rock allowed

What would Jerry Lee Lewis and Chuck Berry (left) have become if fate hadn't intervened? Would they have eclipsed Elvis Presley? Berry's influence turned out to be much more durable than the King's in that the majority of British groups of the sixties, notably the Beatles and the Rolling Stones, started their careers by performing his songs. The chord progressions he devised in the fifties still serve as the reference point for all apprentice rockers.

Throwing out the years of power exercised by old, corrupt and reactionary politicians, in 1960 young America elected to the presidency a man with star quality: John F. Kennedy. His assassination in 1963 coincided with the emergence of the protest song, the first sign of rock's anti-establishment activity.

...presenting t

RON

featuring VER

young people to escape the great postwar ice age. In celebrating youth and its hopes, it had in one sense prepared the way for John F. Kennedy's election in November 1960.

Teenyboppers and bobby-soxers

Women were virtually absent from the ranks of the pioneers of rock and roll. Only Brenda Lee would be part of the early story with 'Sweet Nothin's' and 'I'm Sorry' in 1960. Hers was a rare example of a successful female solo career in a world dominated by men. The female role models of this period, such as Brigitte Bardot, were to be found in the film world, particularly French cinema. Rock was a man's business, because men alone could indulge in tough-guy poses, beyond the taboos of sex and drugs. In this clearly defined universe, Brenda Lee presented the image of a slightly nervous and terribly virginal college girl.

Music would evolve at the beginning of the sixties, thanks to two influential men: Phil Spector in California and George 'Shadow' Morton in New York. Spector invented the 'wall of sound', a recording technique that earned him an uninterrupted succession of spots at the top of the hit parade. With a nod to the modern age, the term is associated with the speed records of the first jet airplanes and with breaking the sound

BE MY BABY

B

C

WHAT'D I S

The Ronettes, with their leader Veronica, nicknamed 'Ronnie' (below).

ETTES

ICA

barrier. Spector gathered as many musicians and singers as he could fit in his studio. By playing with echo chambers and multitracking, he obtained an orchestral intensity that recalled that of a church packed to the rafters on a gospel Sunday.

The artists Phil Spector produced were primarily female groups, beauties like the Crystals ('Da Doo Ron Ron') and the Ronettes ('Be My Baby'), whose leader, Veronica, he married. With Spector and his creation of a sonic language specific to each artist, rock production definitively left the Dark Ages.

At the same time 'Shadow' Morton made a name for himself as another pioneer of production with his favourite group, the Shangri-las. They were white, lived in Queens, New York, and displayed a far more provocative image than, for instance, the innocent Brenda Lee. These girls sang of complicated – and tragic – love affairs with motorcycle gang members ('Leader of the Pack') and, in real life, led an existence worthy of a Jerry Lee Lewis.

Rock and roll arrives in Britain

Since 1956 rock and roll had been very successful in Europe. It was spread by the jukebox and by the movies – *Blackboard Jungle*, with Bill Haley's music, and the first films of Elvis Presley (*King Creole* and *Jailhouse Rock,* the only ones worthy of interest). Radio Luxembourg, with its huge radio transmitter, broadcast the music around the continent.

They were called teenyboppers or bobby-soxers. The girls of rock were pretty and a little seductive, perhaps, but not provocative. Social pressure prohibited them from assuming the suggestive poses of their male counterparts.

Tours by Fats Domino, Little Richard, Eddie Cochran and Gene Vincent generated in their wake a passion that translated itself into the creation of numerous imitations, particularly in Britain. Not only did Britain share a language with the United States, of course, but it had a working-class base with a strong and rebellious identity. A new character appeared on the European scene: the rocker.

In the 1950s anything from America fascinated Europeans. American clothes, films, records and even attitudes constituted symbols of freedom; identifying with this message, European teenagers developed an intense desire to appropriate. Thus, the first British rock singers conformed to their American models quite closely – so much so that they were like copies. Elvis or Gene Vincent could be identified in Tommy Steele ('Singing the Blues'), Billy Fury, Marty Wilde or Rory Storm. The imagery of rock revolved completely around violence, more theatrical than real, which, when it was mixed with British eccentricity, gave rise to a Wee Willie Harris, whose dyed red pile of abundantly brilliantined hair would have appealed to Little Richard.

Another Richard very quickly won the public's favour. Cliff Richard shared similar religious inclinations as his namesake, but in a minor way, remaining true to the 'coolness' displayed by white American rockers. He was certainly a good singer ('Living Doll'), but he was

In Britain at the end of the fifties, the 'teddy boys' (above) adopted elegant attire inspired by the standards of King Edward VII. Coming together in clubs, teddy boys added a new dimension to rockabilly, which had just landed in Britain.

With the twist, popularized by Chubby Checker in his famous 'Let's Twist Again', everyone invented their own steps and danced alone. Pope John XXIII condemned this trend when it made its appearance in Europe at the beginning of the sixties.

above all a stylist inspired by the 'soft' Presley of the Parker years. His performances, however, never overshadowed that of the Shadows, who played with him. Sometimes led by their guitarist, Hank Marvin, a Buddy Holly imitator, the Shadows recaptured the sound of the Ventures, a Seattle group. At the end of the fifties, the Ventures had introduced a new style of electric guitar, brilliant, individual, with a distinctive tremolo sound. The most famous songs by Hank Marvin and the Shadows – without Cliff Richard – ('Apache', 'Kon Tiki') attracted the attention of a public previously hesitant in its response to amplified instruments. Watching Hank Marvin and the Shadows on British television, a number

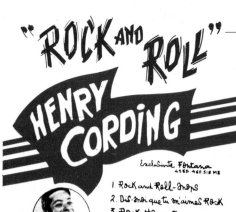

"ROCK AND ROLL"

HENRY CORDING

Exclusivité Fontana
45EP 460.518 ME

1. Rock and Roll-Mops
2. Dis-moi que tu m'aimes ROCK
3. ROCK-Hoquet
4. Va t'faire cuire un Oeuf, man!

et la voix de HENRI SALVADOR

French musicians Boris Vian (above) and Henri Salvador (below) were devoted to jazz but did not ignore rock and roll.

of future 'guitar heroes' saw the birth of their dreams.

The birth of 'yaourt'

On the European continent, in France, rock and roll was at first perceived as a gag, a new manifestation of the impulsive American character. Musicians with strong roots in jazz, like Boris Vian and Henri Salvador, saw in rock a drifting away from the vividness of the blues. They translated their feelings into deliberately idiotic songs like 'Rock 'n' Roll Mops' or 'Va T'Faire Cuire un Oeuf, Man' ('Go Cook an Egg, Man' or 'Get Lost, Man'). None of the early French rockers had an easy time. No one took them seriously, except themselves.

Many French people, however, were ready to buy the American 45s they found in NATO base PXs or the rare French record stores that distributed them. For want of other source materials, several French singers launched into the great adventure of rock and roll by adapting, often colourfully, the gestures and the words of the originals. Thus 'yaourt' ('yogurt') was born, a phonetic caricature of English that tried to recreate an English that very few really understood. The words and meaning didn't matter. Only the spirit counted – and the attitude.

Danyel Gérard was the first champion of this somewhat specialized form of rock. His late-fifties shows recalled those of Johnnie Ray, a pre-Elvis performer who mimicked poses that imitated practices found in American black churches. The press didn't let Gérard get away with it, describing him as a 'suffocating singer'. Then the army grabbed him and destroyed his fledgling career by calling him to serve his country.

The appearance of rock and roll in France did not please everyone. Some laughed at it; others tried to suppress it. And the concerts turned into mayhem. The Palais des Sports arena in Paris was devastated several times, notably in 1961 during performances by Eddie Mitchell et Ses Chaussettes Noires and then again when the band joined Vince Taylor.

A new dance and a new kind of hoodlum

In 1960 the action was situated around the Golf Drouot club in Paris. All of rock's upper crust paraded through there: Johnny Hallyday ('Souvenirs, Souvenirs'), a child of the theatre who modelled himself on the personalities of James Dean and Elvis Presley; Eddie Mitchell et Ses Chaussettes Noires (and His Black Socks), inspired by Gene Vincent's Blue Caps; Danny Boy et les Penitents, Danny Logan et les Pirates, Long Chris et les Daltons. Many of these names were dug up from westerns and comic books, a key part of

TWIST

French teenage culture. In the south of France, Dick Rivers and Ses Chats Sauvages (His Wild Cats) picked up fragments of rock and roll from the American base in Villefranche.

Soon the French discovered the twist, given a place of honour by Chubby Checker. It was a true revolution for dancers:

Eddie Mitchell's Chaussettes Noires and Dick Rivers' Chats Sauvages vied for the favour of the French public. It is to Rivers' credit that 'Twist à Saint Tropez' is considered one of the rare successes of the first wave of French rock.

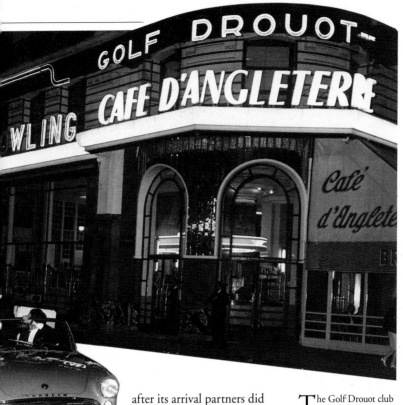

after its arrival partners did
not touch.

The French media – like the
American – was only too glad
to focus on the occasional outburst
of violence. It came as a reminder that this rock and roll
movement was born of an immense frustration with a
terribly restrictive political and social era. There were
many gleeful reports of the devastation of a concert hall
during a concert by the Chaussettes Noires (at this time
led by Vince Taylor), and other articles raised the spectre
of a new kind of hoodlum – called the *blousons noirs* –
leatherclad bullies à la Brando who terrified the French
middle class.

Gone were the old gangs; France had discovered a
new generation of toughs.

The Golf Drouot club
in Paris saw a parade
of the stars of the day and
the hopes of tomorrow. A
kind of amateur talent
show was born here in
front of a jukebox playing
the original versions of
rock and roll songs,
which were remade
into 'yaourt'.

'Hello Friends'

Show business moguls in France quickly realized the
commercial potential represented by the new generation,
and they launched band after band – as well as a series
of solo male and female singers – without regard for
their talent. They Frenchified everything that crossed
the Atlantic. While it was necessary to respect
government-enforced protectionist quotas, the brand-
new station Radio Europe 1 did manage to broadcast
original rock as well as the 'translated' version.

With his radio show, 'Salut Les Copains' ('Hello
Friends'), host Daniel Filipacchi – originally a jazz
critic – recognized the importance of his young
audience and decided to create a magazine for this public.
Conceived in June 1962 in the same spirit as the radio
programme, the magazine gave French teenagers a mirror
that reflected both themselves and their ideals – Johnny
Hallyday, Sylvie Vartan, Françoise Hardy, Richard
Anthony, Sheila – and was such a success that it allowed
Filipacchi to lay the foundations of what would become a
communications empire.

The advent of 'ye-ye'

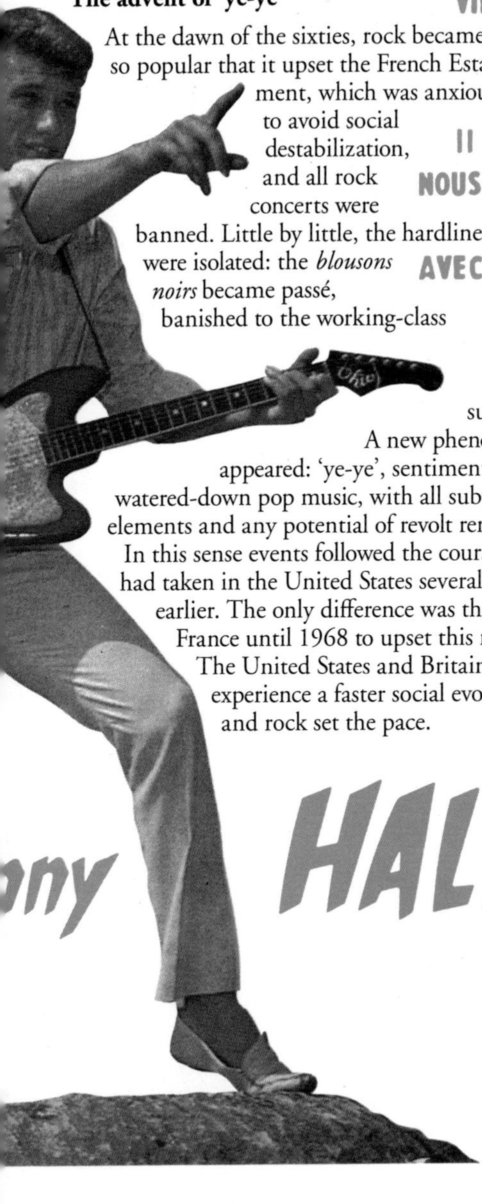

At the dawn of the sixties, rock became so popular that it upset the French Establishment, which was anxious to avoid social destabilization, and all rock concerts were banned. Little by little, the hardliners were isolated: the *blousons noirs* became passé, banished to the working-class suburbs. A new phenomenon appeared: 'ye-ye', sentimental, watered-down pop music, with all subversive elements and any potential of revolt removed. In this sense events followed the course they had taken in the United States several years earlier. The only difference was that it took France until 1968 to upset this new order. The United States and Britain would experience a faster social evolution, and rock set the pace.

VIENS DANSER LE TWIST
Partie 1 en Français
Partie 2 en Anglais
DOUCE VIOLENCE
II FAUT SAISIR SA CHANCE
NOUS, QUAND ON S'EMBRASSE
TOI QUI REGRETTES
AVEC UNE POIGNÉE DE TERRE
TU PEUX LA PRENDRE

In 1961 French rock groups compensated for a dearth of talent with enthusiasm, and the liveliness of the performances made people forget the second-rate music.

HALLYDAY

To the foreigner, Johnny Hallyday personified French rock and roll. One of his first 33 rpm 12" albums celebrated the arrival of the twist in France (left and above).

In the United States rock and roll came from the provinces. And in Britain, too, part of rock's allure was its distinct freshness. The Beatles emerged from Liverpool with their Mersey accents intact on their records. The imagination of a new generation caught fire, and thousands of other groups rushed in.

CHAPTER 3

ROCK WITH AN ENGLISH ACCENT

In Brighton, rockers (left) and the mods of Carnaby Street clashed during the spring of 1964. The mods came out on top in this dispute over clothing, music and style.

Liverpool 1960. As a seaport serving America, Liverpool picked up the new rhythm and blues releases from sailors, before the rest of Britain caught on. Little by little, local groups abandoned 'skiffle', a kind of hillbilly blues born in the Depression years in America and later assimilated in Britain. Lonnie Donegan, its most famous practitioner, was taught by Chris Barber, the leading light of 'trad', the British version of the New Orleans sound and a central figure at the Marquee Club in London. John Lennon was one of Donegan's most devoted followers at the end of the fifties.

Liverpool and the Beatles

In 1957 Lennon asked Paul McCartney to join his group, the Quarrymen, after having heard him perform a spirited version of Eddie Cochran's 'Twenty Flight Rock'. About a year later

THE BEATLES

Brian Epstein (below left) discovered the Beatles in their regular Liverpool club, the Cavern. Attracted first by the personality of John Lennon, Epstein had a decisive influence on the group. His first requirement would be to eliminate the slightly seedy rocker look of the four young men, dressing them up in much more banal outfits than their old leather jackets. Moving into the mainstream, the Beatles recorded their first hits. 'Please Please Me' (the single was released in January 1963) was a clear call for affection to which there was a tremendous public response.

FROM ME TO YOU
ASK ME WHY
I SAW HER STANDING THERE
PLEASE PLEASE ME

McCartney brought in his younger friend George Harrison. Stuart Sutcliffe then joined to play bass, and the group was completed by Pete Best, a drummer. The Quarrymen (the name referred to the Quarry Bank School, which John attended) became Johnny and the Moondogs, then the Silver Beatles – these lengthy names were in honour of Buddy Holly and the Crickets. When the group finally agreed on the name of the Beatles in 1960, it was still a tribute to Holly, with a bit of John Lennon–style wordplay on the word 'beat'.

The band often played at the Cavern, a small underground club in Liverpool. They also toured Germany, performing in the disreputable clubs of the Reeperbahn in Hamburg. There, the group's bassist, Stuart Sutcliffe (who died a few months later), fell in love with photographer Astrid Kirchherr. It was she who had

Australian photographer Robert Freeman posed the Beatles like true icons. The picture above, taken in 1963, which appeared on the cover of their second British album, *With the Beatles*, would remain symbolic of the Beatles' style. Their haircuts marked the starting point for the liberation of hairstyles for all rock artists to come.

suggested that the Beatles adopt their 'French cut' hair style, a kind of wink at French New Wave cinema actors.

Brian Epstein, the biggest record dealer in Liverpool, became the band's manager in late 1961. His first action was to replace Pete Best with Richard Starkey – known as Ringo Starr – the ex-drummer for Rory Storm and the Hurricanes. The magic quartet was now in place.

Beatlemania sweeps the world

Their first album (*Please Please Me*, May 1963) reflected the band's influences: vocal harmonies borrowed from the Everly Brothers, guitar riffs taken from Chuck Berry, spirited melodies recalling Buddy Holly and a falsetto straight from Little Richard. The lyrics, performed in a delightful Liverpudlian accent, addressed themselves directly to the audience ('Love Me Do', 'I Wanna Be Your Man', 'Hold Me Tight', 'I Wanna Hold Your Hand'). The Beatles' popularity grew, and their songs, signed 'Lennon-McCartney', replaced the American standards of rock and rhythm and blues.

The Beatles' success encouraged Brian Epstein to launch a string of groups under the aegis of his company, Northern Songs. Known as the Mersey Beat or the Mersey Sound (after the river that flows through Liverpool), this movement brought to the stage, among others, Gerry and the Pacemakers and Cilla Black – one of the rare female performers of the period.

TO HOLD YOUR HAND • IT WON'T BE LONG
'A BE YOUR MAN • TILL THERE WAS YOU

The Beatles (left) were often forced to pose with backdrops of dubious taste and would soon tire of the servitude imposed on them by promotional campaigns. Their fans ignored these torments and noisily showed their enthusiasm during concerts (below). The music and the words of the songs were lost in the pandemonium. What did it matter? What counted was seeing the Fab Four.

In 1961 the Beatles stayed in Hamburg. Photographer Astrid Kirchherr took their portrait (opposite above) and fell in love with bassist Stuart Sutcliffe. At the time of the photograph there were five Beatles (left to right: Pete Best, George Harrison, John Lennon, Paul McCartney and Stuart Sutcliffe). The group of three guitarists (left) recalled the Shadows, the obligatory reference point of British rock in this period. John Lennon was the only one who possessed an instrument of any value, a Rickenbacker that would later become the Beatles' emblematic guitar. Two years later, reduced to a quartet, they completely revised their look (below). The black-jacketed toughs of Hamburg had become chic young men. By this point they were already very popular, but they returned to Liverpool to play at the Cavern, the little club where they began. Despite its fame, the Cavern would be demolished. However, a museum, statues and several street names perpetuate the memory of the Fab Four in their home town.

THE **BEATLES** ARE AT **THE CAVERN** TUESDAY NIGHT 19TH FEBRUARY 1963 BE EARLY

In 1963 the Beatles turned a corner, and the craziness of Beatlemania began. Their concerts were chaos. People dressed like them and cut their hair like them. The tremendous willingness for change that was in the air – the desire to throw out old Victorian England completely – was incarnated in the Fab Four. Their 45s sold in the millions. Soon Britain was too narrow to contain Beatlemania, and the phenomenon left to conquer the rest of Europe and then the United States.

Blues with a British accent

During this time, there was an influx of blues influence in London as musicians Big Bill Broonzy, Muddy Waters and Sonny Boy Williamson performed. Mick Jagger, Charlie Watts, Jack Bruce and Ginger Baker – in fact, all the key names who would create rock music in the coming years – heard American blues and also gravitated towards British blues musicians Alexis Korner and Cyril Davies.

Like Korner, John Mayall worked hard to respect the spirit and the letter of the blues masters. Eric Clapton, Peter Green, John McVie, Mick Taylor – all 'graduates' of Mayall's Bluesbreakers band – would never forget their lessons. Along with their teacher, they were responsible for the mid-sixties blues boom. And an offspring of Alexis Korner's Blues Incorporated, the Rolling Stones (named after a Muddy Waters song) went on to make rock and roll history.

Keith Richards and Mick Jagger had known each other since childhood. They shared with Brian Jones, whom they met at Korner's, a pronounced taste for rhythm and blues in all its forms: the image-filled vitality of street language, a nonchalant attitude, and extravagant hair and dress. Jagger revelled in the pleasure of the music, outdoing Presley and his famous swagger. The Stones' first manager, Andrew Loog Oldham, encouraged them, thinking that their style would at least distinguish them from the 'nice' Beatles.

The Rolling Stones

On their first album (*The Rolling Stones*) the Stones paid an emphatic compliment to those who influenced them, in particular

The first Rolling Stones album (above), released in 1964, was a direct homage to Chuck Berry. The contrast with the Beatles – their real or supposed rivals – was striking. Abandoning their stage costumes and smiles, they followed the advice of their manager, Andrew Loog Oldham: to speak frankly, to make no concessions to photographers and, under all circumstances, to give the impression of being bored and outraged.

The Rolling Stones in 1964 (left). Left to right: Brian Jones, Charlie Watts, Mick Jagger and Keith Richards. And a year later in 1965 (opposite).

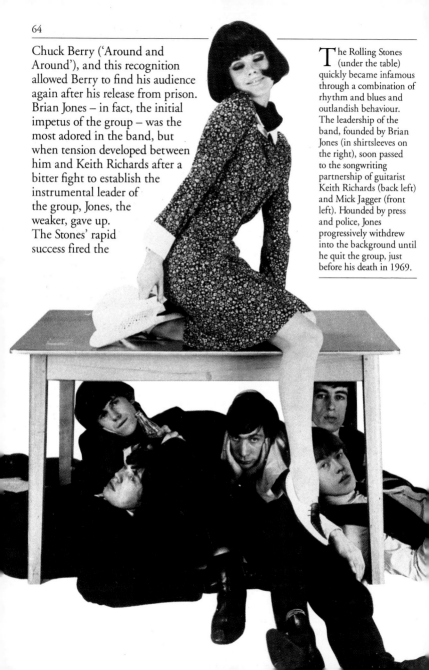

Chuck Berry ('Around and Around'), and this recognition allowed Berry to find his audience again after his release from prison. Brian Jones – in fact, the initial impetus of the group – was the most adored in the band, but when tension developed between him and Keith Richards after a bitter fight to establish the instrumental leader of the group, Jones, the weaker, gave up. The Stones' rapid success fired the

The Rolling Stones (under the table) quickly became infamous through a combination of rhythm and blues and outlandish behaviour. The leadership of the band, founded by Brian Jones (in shirtsleeves on the right), soon passed to the songwriting partnership of guitarist Keith Richards (back left) and Mick Jagger (front left). Hounded by press and police, Jones progressively withdrew into the background until he quit the group, just before his death in 1969.

rhythm and blues movement in Britain. Groups exploded from every corner.

In London the Pretty Things were formed around Dick Taylor, a member of the first Stones lineup. The Yardbirds, a younger, pure blues–based group, saw a parade of three legendary guitarists: Eric Clapton, the first 'guitar hero', who was nicknamed God by his fans and left the group when it became popular ('For Your Love'); Jeff Beck, who reinvented the electric guitar by integrating into his technique a sludge of sound – especially fuzz and distortion ('Shapes of Things'); and Jimmy Page, who attended the creation of most of the great hits of the era.

In Newcastle the Animals, with their singer Eric Burdon, came to prominence with recordings such as 'House of the Rising Sun', influenced by Bob Dylan. In Ireland the group Them, featuring singer Van Morrison, championed a rough rhythm and blues ('Gloria'). They all shared a passion for black American music, to which they brought a distinctly British sensibility and, of course, flamboyant look which would help turn many into world-beaters.

T he Pretty Things (above) never achieved the same success as the Rolling Stones. In fact, their leader, Dick Taylor (second from the right), had been the original bassist for the Stones during their early days in 1962.

Mods and rockers

British rock didn't just sell records. It was a tremendous promotional tool for other products: miniskirts and cosmetics (Mary Quant), hair salons (Vidal Sassoon), boots, costumes. But beyond the emphasis on dress, the entire society was in the process of shifting, turning its back on outdated customs. These upheavals did not please everyone.

Lovers of pure rock and roll felt the original message was degraded and the raw energy of the pioneers of the genre was diluted. They maintained that distinctive look: exaggerated pompadours, sideburns, leather jackets and big British motorcycles. Rooted in the 1950s, the rockers regularly confronted their opposites, the mods, who were aggressively up to date, with their short hair, French clothes and decorated motor scooters. It was Carnaby Street, the fashionable London district, versus Club 59. Symbolically, the split between the two movements occurred in 1962 when Pete Best was dismissed from the Beatles because of his refusal to change, to adopt a new image.

First, you had to be cool, aloof. The mods were the first to claim the use of legally suspect substances, particularly amphetamines ('purple hearts'), which they took to enable them to dance all through the weekend. The long hot summer was punctuated with their pitched battles against the rockers in the wild clubs of Soho and on the beaches of Brighton. Inevitably, the mods won. They discovered economic independence and all its available pleasures. Their musical tastes tended towards modern jazz (hence their name) and classic rhythm and blues, which they danced to on the weekends. The Who, originally named High Numbers, expressed some of the mod credos in their songs: 'My Generation' with its swaggering refrain ('Hope I die before I get old') or 'Pictures of Lily', an ode to masturbation.

In 1963 the motorcyclists of Club 59 on British Nortons and Triumphs confronted the wave of mods perched on decorated Italian motor scooters (above). Added to this contest of machinery was a profound difference in musical taste. The motorcyclists – or rockers (opposite above) – supported the rock and roll of the fifties, while the mods preferred the new English groups, above all the Who, whose clothing was mod in inspiration.

Who Put The Bomp

VOLUME 3 NO. 1   HOLLYWOOD, CALIFORNIA   BUY BONDS   FALL 1973   PRICE $1.00

BRITISH INVASION

The British Invasion

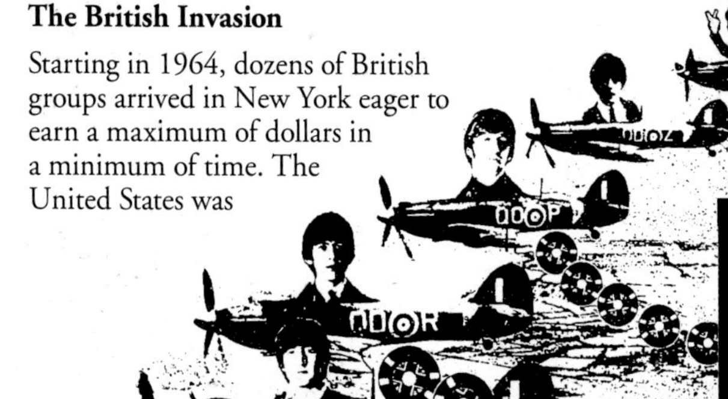

Starting in 1964, dozens of British
groups arrived in New York eager to
earn a maximum of dollars in
a minimum of time. The
United States was

It's time
we exorcise
this demon
influence
over our
children

at their mercy. It had not seen such
enthusiasm since the golden days
of rock and roll. Welcomed by the media, the
Beatles outsmarted every trap set by interviewers by
their use of humour. Now there were the same scenes
of hysteria in the United States as in Britain – delirious
girls, hotels taken by storm and 'authentic' souvenir
businesses selling shreds of sheets that were worn around
the neck like religious emblems, autographs scribbled by
bodyguards or, on a higher level, tea sets and wallpapers.
In the second wave the Rolling Stones provoked similar
riots. Mick Jagger's very physical stage performance

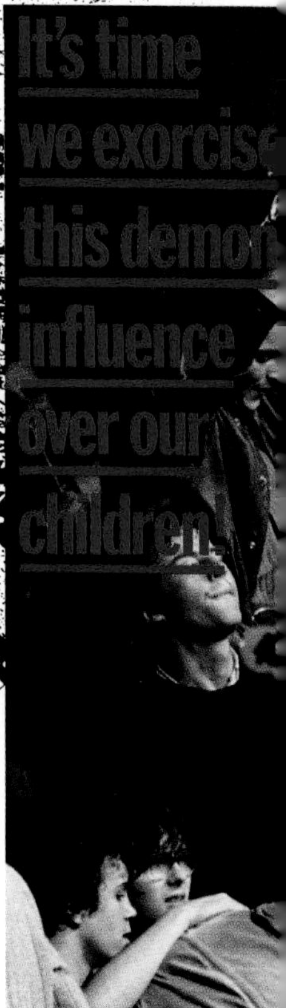

completely changed the former attitude of white American singers. Most of them now wanted to imitate his leaps and his catlike poses.

But it was in its impact on society that the 'British Invasion' produced its most remarkable effect. Beatnik America recognized itself in these young rebels, especially since they were held in contempt by the Establishment. The entire country was traumatized by John Kennedy's assassination. And the British tornado stimulated the energies of a new generation of artists – rockers, poets, singers – who seemed to have been waiting just for this opportunity to express themselves.

More than ten years after the beginning of the British Invasion, *Who Put The Bomp*, an American rock fanzine (opposite), recalled the important role of the Beatles and the Rolling Stones (below, in concert in 1970).

In the early sixties, the youth of America underwent a profound moral crisis. The Vietnam War, the civil rights movement and the corruption of the political and legal system led to strong anti-establishment sentiment and general unrest. Rock and roll musicians suddenly took on an unprecedented role: they became the spokespeople of a generation. In the forefront was Bob Dylan.

CHAPTER 4

AN AMERICAN REVOLUTION

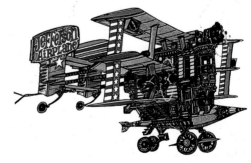

After the first wave of protest songs, rock discovered political commitment. Propelled by the music of bands like the Jefferson Airplane, anti-establishment and anti-war activity pervaded college campuses.

The rhythm and blues music that had provided such glorious times for the British mods was created in the hit factories of Motown in Detroit and Stax in Memphis. Motown, founded by Berry Gordy in 1959, produced Marvin Gaye ('Ain't That Peculiar'),

Smokey Robinson ('I Second that Emotion'), the Temptations ('Ain't Too Proud to Beg'), the Four Tops ('Bernadette'), Stevie Wonder ('Fingertips – Part 2'), the Jackson Five ('ABC'), Diana Ross and the Supremes ('Where Did Our Love Go?'), Martha and the Vandellas ('Dancing in the Streets'), Gladys Knight and the Pips ('I Heard It Through the Grapevine') and others. In ten years over a hundred Motown songs made number one on the hit parade.

Stax, however, was tough competition. Their

While the Beatles and the Rolling Stones dominated Europe, America supported such black rhythm and blues artists as Otis Redding (below), Al Green and the stars of the Motown stable (above).

legendary rhythm section – Booker T. Jones (the composer of 'Green Onions', at the Hammond organ) and his MGs (who would later play with the Blues Brothers) – accompanied such house artists as Otis Redding ('Try a Little Tenderness'), without doubt one of the great soul singers of his generation, and Sam and Dave ('Hold On, I'm Coming'). The Stax studio enjoyed such a reputation that Atlantic Records, its distributor, recorded its own artists, like Wilson Pickett ('In the Midnight Hour'), in the Memphis studio. But of all the black singers, James Brown had the greatest success. Celebrated as 'the hardest- working man in

Detroit, the car capital of America, was the home of Motown, the birthplace of countless hits. Among its stars were the Jackson Five (below, Michael, age eight, is at the bottom in the centre).

showbusiness', Brown was an innovator as well as a model showman. He was an amazing dancer, constantly inventing new steps (enumerated in his song 'Papa's Got a Brand New Bag'). He influenced his American colleagues (like Michael Jackson) as much as British pop groups. The Apollo Theater in Harlem, New York, was the scene of many of his greatest performances.

Gospel: the unique crucible

Former preachers like Al Green ('I Can't Get Next to You') or children of pastors like Aretha Franklin ('Respect') learned to sing in church, and in their careers they maintained a religious current in rock and in rhythm and blues through their song lyrics, with their optimism, their hope for a better world and their messages bordering on prayer.

74

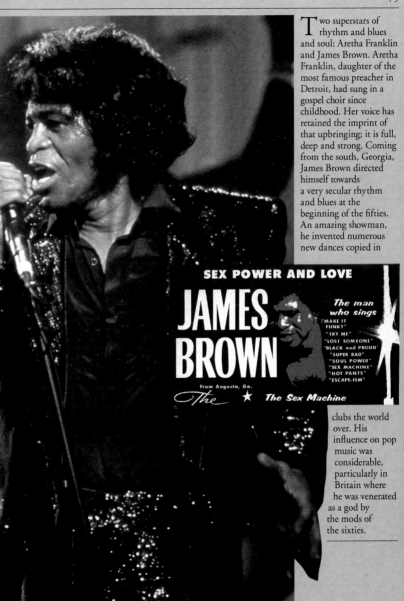

Two superstars of rhythm and blues and soul: Aretha Franklin and James Brown. Aretha Franklin, daughter of the most famous preacher in Detroit, had sung in a gospel choir since childhood. Her voice has retained the imprint of that upbringing; it is full, deep and strong. Coming from the south, Georgia, James Brown directed himself towards a very secular rhythm and blues at the beginning of the fifties. An amazing showman, he invented numerous new dances copied in

SEX POWER AND LOVE

JAMES BROWN

From Augusta, Ga.

The ★ The Sex Machine

The man who sings
"MAKE IT FUNKY"
"TRY ME"
"LOST SOMEONE"
'BLACK and PROUD'
"SUPER BAD"
"SOUL POWER"
"SEX MACHINE"
"HOT PANTS"
"ESCAPE-ISM"

clubs the world over. His influence on pop music was considerable, particularly in Britain where he was venerated as a god by the mods of the sixties.

This feeling has also manifested itself in the fever generated by some concerts, their ritualization and, in recent years, their focus on great humanitarian causes.

At the beginning of the sixties, this current of devotion found a renewed interest among whites with the protest song. Rooted partially in folk, bluegrass and blues, as well as in gospel, the movement focused as much on the spiritual as on the political. Led by Pete Seeger and his 'Sing Out' revue, folk singers devoted themselves to challenging institutions and consciousness raising in general. The most remarkable performers were Phil Ochs, Eric Andersen, Peter, Paul and Mary, and, above all, Joan Baez and Bob Dylan.

Bob Dylan: rock becomes literary

When Bob Dylan's first album appeared in 1962, folk was already in fashion on college campuses. The Kingston Trio ('Tom Dooley') and the

In 1965 Richard Avedon took this fine portrait of Joan Baez (above) for her album *Farewell, Angelina*. The title song was written by Bob Dylan (opposite), who was then sharing her life. Labelled 'the king and queen of folk' by the media, Dylan and Baez spoke for the hopes of the public.

Joan Baez (left, at the microphone) was a key participant in political events, here seen as part of the Free Speech Movement – against censorship and for the freedom of speech – on the Berkeley campus of the University of California in 1963.

Brothers Four ('Greenfields') concentrated on poignant songs, rich in vocal harmonies but non-threatening to the Establishment.

But Dylan made his reputation as a rebel. Born Robert Zimmerman, 24 May 1941, in Duluth, Minnesota, he was influenced early on by the rock and roll of Little Richard, the country and western of Hank Williams and the whole persona of Woody Guthrie. Everything about Guthrie fascinated him: the writer-hobo precursor of Kerouac, the protest singer who translated the tragedies of ruined farmers and tramps into songs, the social commentator, the wounded hero, the vagabond. The first success of Bob Dylan carried the imprint of this relationship. Dubbed by Pete Seeger the authentic heir to Woody Guthrie, Dylan, who could have contented himself to be the darling of student rebels, established himself as a redresser of wrongs and then became larger than life, a widely imitated prophet.

Summer of 1965: the Newport Folk Festival

To the great dismay of folk purists, Dylan appeared onstage with an electric guitar, accompanied by the Butterfield Blues Band. It was a typical rock and roll challenge, especially since he seemed to have renounced plaid shirts for a look borrowed from the Beatles.

Dylan continued along his path as an absolute individualist. Encouraged by his producer Tom Wilson, he intensified his exploration of rock in a remarkable two years, 1965–6, marked by three key albums. The half-acoustic,

Bob Dylan's acoustic guitar remained a painful symbol in the hearts of folk lovers. For them, Dylan was the emblematic figure of the protest song, heir to Woody Guthrie, charged with a messianic task, which he never ceased to refuse ('Don't follow leaders!' he wrote in 1965). Purists needed years to accept Dylan's electric arrangements and heated rock and roll exchanges. As if to disconcert his audience again and again, he would periodically return to his original style.

BC

first and only has area performance

half-electric *Bringing It All Back Home* and *Highway 61 Revisited*, shot through by the lightning streaks of Mike Bloomfield's guitar, were both produced by Wilson and released in 1965. *Blonde on Blonde* (1966), the first double album in the history of rock, was recorded in Nashville, the centre of country music. These records were studded with such classic cuts as 'Like a Rolling Stone'. In the mid-sixties Dylan also toured with the Band, critically acclaimed and influential in their own right.

DYLAN

saturday, february 22, 8:30 p.m.

berkeley community theater

admission: $2.50, 3.00, & 3.75

Bob Dylan concerts sometimes turned unruly. In 1965 at the Newport Folk Festival the audience booed him. He had dared to venture on stage accompanied by a blues-rock group, the Butterfield Blues Band. In the spring of 1966 an equally stormy welcome awaited him

The invention of California

By 1966 America had found a credible reply to

in music concert
a folk

at the Royal Albert Hall in London, where supporters and adversaries of the 'new' Dylan confronted each other.

GIRLS ON THE BEACH

the Beatles: the Beach Boys. The Wilson brothers – Brian, Carl and Dennis – their cousin Mike Love and their friend Al Jardine landed their first hit in 1961 with 'Surfin'. Dennis was the only surfer in the band, but he persuaded Brian, an enormously talented lyricist and composer, to write songs glorifying the pleasures preferred by his friends: dune buggies, girls and the beach. The 'surf sound' was born at the same time as the myth of a carefree, sunny California, a teenager's green paradise, complete with dragsters and dark suntans. Something in Brian Wilson's songs conveyed the feeling of Chuck Berry during his 'School Day' era. This rhythm, blended with complex vocal harmonies inherited from the Everly Brothers and the Four Freshmen, propelled the Beach Boys to the head of American groups. Other Californian bands included the Mamas and the Papas ('California Dreamin'), the Turtles ('Happy Together'), Buffalo Springfield (with Stephen Stills and Neil Young, 'For What It's Worth') and the Byrds (with Roger McGuinn and David Crosby, 'Eight Miles High').

Los Angeles, of course, didn't tell the whole Californian story. As the wind of psychedelia began to blow, San Francisco, with its reputation for tolerance, seemed infinitely hipper. And, mid-decade, the term 'hippies' was born. At the beginning, hippies, heirs to the beatniks, were primarily intellectuals who turned their back on the Establishment's power game and competition. The news gradually spread across America

The Beach Boys (opposite) strutted about, posing as surfers for the camera. In reality, only the drummer, Dennis Wilson (first in line) surfed. His brother Brian (last in line) was the soul of the group. He lived by himself and composed his hymns to the pleasures of adolescence – girls, cars and surfing – based on Dennis' adventures.

In 1967 Joan Baez participated in a protest in front of an armed forces recruitment centre in Oakland, California. A pacifist, she advocated non-violence.

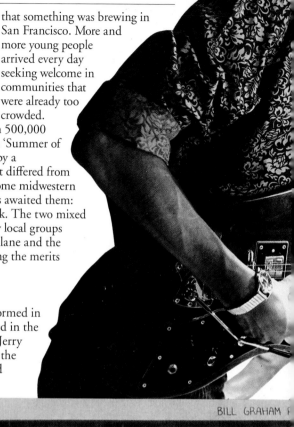

that something was brewing in San Francisco. More and more young people arrived every day seeking welcome in communities that were already too crowded.

There were more than 500,000 'runaways' during the 'Summer of Love' (1967), drawn by a perspective on life that differed from what was offered in some midwestern suburb. Two products awaited them: acid – LSD – and rock. The two mixed happily, with songs by local groups like the Jefferson Airplane and the Grateful Dead extolling the merits of acid 'trips'.

Psychedelic rock

The Grateful Dead, formed in late 1965, was crowned in the glory of the pioneers. Jerry Garcia, spokesman of the group, was nicknamed

BILL GRAHAM

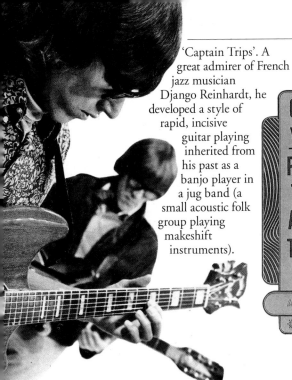

'Captain Trips'. A great admirer of French jazz musician Django Reinhardt, he developed a style of rapid, incisive guitar playing inherited from his past as a banjo player in a jug band (a small acoustic folk group playing makeshift instruments).

Centre, left and right: Jorma Kaukonen and Paul Kantner, cofounders of the Jefferson Airplane.

CAN
YOU
PASS
THE
ACID
TEST
?

The Grateful Dead and the Jefferson Airplane toured North America in 1967 (poster below).

THE SAN FRANCISCO SCENE

GRATEFUL DEAD

TORONTO
TO
AUG 5

LIGHT SHOW BY HEAD LIGHTS

CENTRE
Mats. Wed & Sat   Box Office Open from 11 am to 9pm.   J.GARDNER

Other members brought with them their individual sounds: Bob Weir, rock and roll; Ron 'Pigpen' McKernan, rhythm and blues; and Phil Lesh, tonal research. Drummer Bill Kreutzmann completed the group. In 1966 the Dead settled down in the eye of the storm on Ashbury Street and participated in all the

The Family Dog (right) was the biggest hippie among the concert promoters.

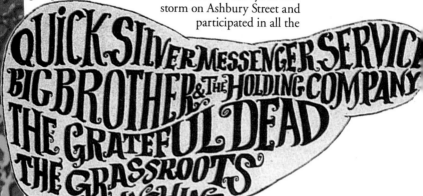

QUICKSILVER MESSENGER SERVICE
BIG BROTHER & THE HOLDING COMPANY
THE GRATEFUL DEAD
THE GRASSROOTS
SUNSHINE

great events of the area, like the famous Human Be-In held in Golden Gate Park in January 1967 and free concerts bringing together the best local groups – Quicksilver Messenger Service ('Happy Trails'), Big Brother and the Holding Company (with its singer Janis

In 1966 San Francisco's Fillmore Auditorium entrusted the creation of its concert posters to the best graphic artists of the day. They tried to outdo each other in presenting the local talent (left and below) as well as touring bands (opposite below, the Yardbirds).

BIG BROTHER AND THE HOLDING COMPANY
FILLMORE AND GEARY 8:00 P.M. FILLMORE AUDITORIUM
SATURDAY FEB. 10

Joplin, 'Cheap Thrills'), the Charlatans ('Charlatans') and the Jefferson Airplane.

The Airplane debuted as a folk-rock group around the same time as the Dead, making their first recording in 1966 with a banjo (Marty Balin), acoustic guitar (Paul Kantner), bass (Bob Harvey), drums (Skip Spence), lead guitar (Jorma Kaukonen) and a singer, Signe Anderson, who quickly gave way to Grace Slick. With its second album, *Surrealistic Pillow*, the Airplane established itself as a leading voice of the hippie movement, its poetic lyrics evoking hallucinogens, free love and social commitment. The band didn't escape the notice of Bill Graham, creator of the legendary concerts at the Fillmore, and the Jefferson Airplane became a major attraction on the San Francisco scene.

Faced with such success, the big recording companies raced each other to sign psychedelic artists. This would be the chance for Big Brother; for Carlos Santana, the Chicano guitarist ('Evil Ways'); and for Country Joe McDonald and the Fish, a band composed of politicized Berkeleyans taking a stand against the Vietnam War ('I-Feel-Like-I'm-Fixin'-To-Die').

Revolution on Sunset Boulevard

In Los Angeles bands proliferated, but their identities stayed more separate than in San Francisco, for there was no cementing force like the hippie movement to bring them together. Here everyone was an individual with individual inspiration and individual talent. Some groups stood out: the Doors (with Jim Morrison), for example, and Frank Zappa, Captain Beefheart ('Trout Mask Replica'), the bluesy Canned Heat ('Goin' Up the Country'), Steppenwolf ('Born to be Wild') and Arthur Lee's Love ('Forever Changes').

The legend of Jim Morrison, singer for the Doors (album cover for *Strange Days* below), began to spread after his death in 1971.

The Doors, who made their debut in 1966, took their name from Aldous Huxley's book *The Doors of Perception*, consecrated to his experience with hallucinogens. Morrison garnered attention because of his provocative stage performance. More than a singer, he wanted to be a poet, a rebel, the conscience of a generation. Supported by solid musicians – notably organist Ray Manzarek – and passionate about European poetry and philosophy, Jim 'the Lizard King' revived the myth of the rock and roll hero, fragile and triumphant, adored by hordes of fans but condemned to inevitable self-destruction. Of all the rock output in those crazy years, the music of the Doors is one of the rare examples to have survived to this day without suffering musically: 'Riders on the Storm', and 'LA Woman', for example.

Zappa and his Mothers

Frank Zappa seemed very different. An erudite musician, he was subject to two major and apparently contradictory influences: black fifties doo-wop and composer Edgard Varèse. Zappa's favourite weapon was Dada-like humour, with references to Groucho Marx, whom he even resembled. Zappa understood that his audience was, like him, breaking its bonds with society. His musicians, the Mothers of Invention, like his entourage, reflected his aspirations. Through his albums Zappa developed the different facets of his inspiration, from the most complex *(Lumpy Gravy, Uncle Meat* and the 1971 film *200 Motels)* to the most openly critical *(We're Only in It for the Money),* to the most frankly parodic *(Cruising with Ruben and the Jets),* performed in a fifties doo-wop style. Obsessed with the official recognition of his status as a contemporary classical composer, he performed the score to *200 Motels* with Zubin Mehta and the Los Angeles Philharmonic in 1970.

Frank Zappa (below), a prolific artist, tried everything: classical music and rock, film and video, and sometimes even politics. In the extravagantly produced *200 Motels,* his first feature film (in which Ringo Starr played the role of Zappa), Zappa cheerfully teased the narrow world of rock. For his third album, *We're Only in It for the Money,* Zappa received authorization from the Beatles to imitate the cover of their famous *Sgt Pepper* album (below left).

FRANK

ZAPPA

Beneath his buffoonish look, Frank Zappa sustained a great interest in very serious music. After his *Lumpy Gravy* album, filled with nods to modern composer Edgard Varèse, Zappa explored in 1969 a more jazzy vein in *Hot Rats* (shown here), accompanied by violinists Jean-Luc Ponty and Don 'Sugarcane' Harris.

Pierre Boulez conducted a symphony orchestra performing his works in the mid-eighties.

Lou Reed and the Velvet Underground

When Frank Zappa arrived in New York in July 1967 to set up his show of surrealist cabaret at the Garrick Theater, the local 'underground' scene was already very strong. The *East Village Other* newspaper drew artists with the same critical approach – notably directed against the Vietnam War, but with a less 'erudite' musical orientation: the Fugs (with poets Tuli Kupferberg and Ed Sanders), the Holy Modal Rounders (with the young Sam

The Velvet Underground at the Dom in New York in 1967 (above), with a light show designed by Andy Warhol.

Shepard), Pearls Before Swine and, a little more removed, the Velvet Underground.

Lou Reed also came from the field of poetry. His meeting with Sterling Morrison and John Cale, highly trained in modern composition, determined the foundation of the Velvet Underground (a name taken from a sado-masochistic novel by Michael Leigh). The group's rough improvisations caused it to be banned from most clubs. Then pop artist Andy Warhol discovered the band. In Warhol's huge studio, the

Factory, Dylan met Edie Sedgwick. The group rehearsed surrounded by Gérard Malanga's silkscreens, various superstars and the actresses known as the Chelsea Girls – Ingrid, Viva, Ultra Violet and Nico (who soon joined the group).

For several months the Velvet Underground performed at the Dom in New York's East Village. Warhol's hand was present even in the show's title – the Exploding Plastic Inevitable. Warhol 'produced' the band's first album (*The Velvet Under-*

ground and Nico, 1967), and, in fact, his presence alone was enough to confer on it a certain aura that others were charged with transferring on to vinyl. The short period of the Velvet Underground (1967–9) profoundly marked pop music. Well after the band broke up, Lou Reed was still seen as the Chuck Berry of the eighties.

Andy Warhol

Andy Warhol's pop art manifested itself in all the activities of the Velvet Underground, such as, for example, the cover of its first album (detail, centre). In the original version, which was released during the summer of 1967, this peel was removable and revealed the naked banana underneath. Today, collectors pay a fortune for this example of a successful collaboration between two artistic worlds.

Nico was a model-starlet when she met Andy Warhol. He made her one of the stars of his 1966 film *Chelsea Girls* and then suggested that Lou Reed entrust her with some vocals for the Velvet Underground. She participated in the band's first album before starting a solo career.

WOODSTOCK
MUSIC & ART FAIR
presents
AN
AQUARIAN
EXPOSITION
in
WHITE LAKE, N.
WITH
FRI., AUG. 15
Joan Baez
Arlo Guthrie
Tim Hardin
Richie Havens
Incredible String Band
Ravi Shankar
Sly And The Family Stone
Bert Sommer
Sweetwater
SAT., AUG. 16
Canned Heat
Creedence Clearwater
Grateful Dead
Keef Hartley
Janis Joplin
Jefferson Airplane
Mountain
Quill
Santana
The Who
SUN., AUG. 17
The Band
Jeff Beck Group
Blood, Sweat and Tears
Joe Cocker
Crosby, Stills and Nash
Jimi Hendrix
Iron Butterfly
Ten Years After
Johnny Winter
AUGUST
15, 16, 17.
3 DAYS
of PEACE
& MUSIC

In 1968 rock and roll was at the heart of a vast cultural and political movement with its performers as its leaders. Rock served as a vehicle for the ideas of love, peace and brotherhood that were being celebrated at giant festivals. But eventually it lost the biting sound that had made it inaccessible to many, and the music business took advantage of a larger and larger audience.

CHAPTER 5

THE VIEW FROM WOODSTOCK

The majority of the names that appeared on this poster for the Woodstock festival were relatively unknown to the general public before the concert. But the media impact of the event was such that in the blink of an eye a number of the artists became superstars. Big Brother and the Holding Company album cover (right).

Psychedelia made its official appearance in Britain in the autumn of 1966, making an indelible mark on the musical world. The whole underground scene revolved around the magazines *IT (International Times)* and *Oz.* Concerts were organized in London at the Roundhouse, the Alexandra Palace and a little club called the UFO. Two groups – Pink Floyd and Soft Machine – played there for the first time.

Rock goes 'cosmic'

Pink Floyd was led by an enraptured dandy, Syd Barrett, joined by three former architectural school students. With birdcalls, industrial noises and

The members of Pink Floyd (above, at the end of the seventies) hid in the background of their stage productions, which were aimed more to seduce than to alarm. But when Syd Barrett (opposite) was in command from 1966 to 1967, he plunged the audience into a climate of anguish far removed from the spirit of the 'good vibrations' of the time.

blinding light shows, the Pink Floyd universe was like a nightmare, with science fiction as the excuse for all the theatrics *(The Piper at the Gates of Dawn)*. After Barrett's departure – he had become mentally ill – guitarist David Gilmour arrived and gave the music its 'cosmic' style *(The Dark Side of the Moon)*. Pink Floyd was an influence on a number of groups.

Another band formed by students, Soft Machine, experienced a different fate. For the mods-become-hippies, the band was the realization of their old dreams of a modern jazz allied to pop culture. The name of the group – a superb underground reference – came from the title of a William Burroughs novel. Soft Machine was very popular in France, and in England the influence of the band's Robert Wyatt was considerable in the development of a progressive rock style; this style gradually separated itself from the traditional patterns of rock and roll. Wyatt left Soft Machine in 1971 after recovering

When Robert Wyatt left Soft Machine, he formed a new group, Matching Mole.

from a difficult album *(Fourth)* and founded the band Matching Mole. He reached the peak of his art in 1974 after an accident left him confined to a wheelchair. Supported by Pink Floyd, he recorded the album *Rock Bottom* (produced by the group's drummer, Nick Mason), seen by some at the time as one of the most original masterpieces in the history of rock.

Following the lead of the progressive, or art-rock, movement, the majority of new musical genres that proliferated in the seventies in Britain dawned between the end of

1966 and the end of 1968. The desire for change, for evolution, manifested itself in a 360-degree search for other sounds, other rhythms, other examples. The British empire was ready to provide a number, thanks primarily to India. In the 1965 song 'Norwegian Wood', George Harrison had introduced the sitar to the music of the Beatles. The great Indian sitar player Ravi Shankar himself advised Harrison, particularly on the recording of *Sgt Pepper* two years later.

Is *Sgt Pepper* a masterpiece? A cornerstone in the history of rock? Or pure megalomania? *Sgt Pepper's Lonely Hearts Club Band*, always a popular and critical success, opened the door to concept albums. After this time (1967) it was possible to spread out on one or more sides of a record in order to develop an idea or create a mini-opera. This genre triumphed in 1969 with the Who and their ambitious rock opera *Tommy*. In the late sixties and early seventies, with operas and symphonies, rock flirted dangerously with a respectable classicism – the Moody Blues *(Days of Future Passed)*, Emerson, Lake and Palmer *(Pictures at*

Soft Machine, 1971 (above, on the cover of their *Third* album). Left to right: Elton Dean, Hugh Hopper, Mike Ratledge and Robert Wyatt. The apparent weariness reflects the tensions that were tearing the four musicians apart; Wyatt left the band a few months later. The humour, fantasy and imagination then disappeared from the music of Soft Machine, giving way to a dull jazz-rock.

an Exhibition), King Crimson *(In the Court of the Crimson King)*. Anything went since the Beatles, encouraged by their producer George Martin, had introduced violins here and a harpsichord there. They were often and quickly imitated by their cousins, the Stones *(Their Satanic Majesties Request)*. Happily, there were still the blues.

Supergroups, megastars, giant festivals

By the end of 1966 the John Mayall–Graham Bond–Alexis Korner matrix had given birth to the first supergroup in history: Cream. The members were Eric Clapton (guitar), Jack Bruce (bass) and Ginger Baker (drums). With their high-volume rock-blues, they announced the intensification of the approach to rock, which later led to hard rock and heavy metal. The power trio had only one serious competitor: the Jimi Hendrix Experience.

Hendrix was American. He made his debut as a guitarist backing Little Richard and Curtis Knight, a rhythm and blues singer. During the summer of 1966, Chas Chandler (the former bassist for the Animals had become a manager) discovered him in a club in Greenwich Village, New York. He brought Hendrix to London and had him record a bluesy version of a standard, 'Hey Joe', which was an immediate success. The music press was completely overwhelmed. There was now another guitar hero besides Clapton to carry out the fusion of the blues currents and psychedelia. Hendrix redefined the instrument, using all available effects to create previously unheard-of sounds. His influence was felt by every guitar player who followed.

at The Boston Tea Pa
with Tony Williams
Tuesday & Wednesday, November 11 & 12
15 Lansdowne St. 536-0915
Lights: Roger Thomas - Tickets: Krackerjack
Headquarters E., George's Folly, New Directi

Valiant warriors of the British Invasion, the Who had a sullied reputation. They ended their concerts by destroying their instruments on stage, they wrecked their hotel rooms and they threw their cars into their hosts' pools. In short, they constituted an extremely bad example for other groups – who hastened to imitate them.

In June 1967 Hendrix was one of the stars of the
Monterey International Pop Festival in California.
His performance remains a legendary moment in
the history of rock concerts. Modest and unpretentious
at first, this small festival was transformed by producer
Lou Adler and John Phillips of the Mamas and the
Papas into a showcase of Californian rock. Janis Joplin,
the Jefferson Airplane and Canned Heat were
discovered there surrounded by Otis Redding, Ravi
Shankar and other key talents of the day. The idea
of more and more elaborate gatherings developed.

Each of Jimi Hendrix's
stage appearances
threw the fundamentals
of rock and roll into
question. He 'slayed' the
electric guitar, like
Charlie Parker 'slayed'
the saxophone.
Performing after such
giants was certainly not
an easy task.

Jimi superstar

Jimi Hendrix was a larger-than-life figure, and all the festivals wanted to include him in their concerts. His guitar playing was enriched by new sounds, while remaining faithful to the spirit of the blues and its twelve-bar structure. His group, the Experience, underwent several transformations. His English back-up, bassist Noel Redding and drummer Mitch Mitchell, gave way to black Americans. His army buddy Billy Cox became bassist, and Buddy Miles, a drummer then much in vogue, joined them. The trio sometimes performed under the name Band of Gypsies. Hendrix hoped thus to reconquer the black audience. It was, however, a crowd of mostly white faces that acclaimed him at the festivals in Monterey in 1967, Woodstock in 1969 and the Isle of Wight in 1969.

Janis Joplin

From 1966 Janis Joplin was a star of the rock scene in San Francisco. She was only twenty-three years old but already possessed solid experience in the blues. Back in her native Texas, she had grown up listening to the records of black artists, above all Bessie Smith. She knew Smith's songs by heart and managed to imitate them with ease, but she could not have known that her destiny would be as tragic as her model's. In San Francisco the popularity of her group, Big Brother and the Holding Company, coincided with the growth of the hippie movement. She reigned at concerts at the Fillmore Auditorium and the Avalon Ballroom, but she lived alone, exploited by drug dealers and duped by her friends — the blues, always the blues. Discovered by Bob Dylan's manager, Albert Grossman, at the Monterey festival, she began a brief solo career which came to an end in 1970 in a motel with a fatal overdose. The legend was born. During the next decade, every female rocker would cite her as a model.

WOODSTOCK MUSIC and ART FAIR
SUNDAY
AUGUST 17, 1969
10:00 A. M.
$7.00 Good For One Admission Only
M 02950
NO REFUNDS GLOBE TICKET COMPANY

The result was Woodstock (the Woodstock Music and Art Fair in White Lake, near Bethel, New York) in August 1969.

Woodstock, vision of history

More than 300,000 people flocked to attend these three famous days of music, peace, love, rain, and drugs. Little-known performers and groups (Richie Havens, Joe Cocker and Ten Years After) found themselves propelled in one stroke to the level of megastars, due to the festival's highly promoted spin-offs (the film, live album and tours).

The music business knew perfectly well how to profit from this fantastic publicity coup. Rock became an industry, with its constraints and its need for expansion. All the hype was successful. Suddenly a group did not count until it had appeared in a giant festival – the Isle of Wight or

The organizers of the Woodstock festival did not expect such a crowd, and they certainly did not expect that the majority of the spectators would enter without paying. Due to the general goodwill of the crowd there was no material damage or physical violence; this was not true of later events of the same type.

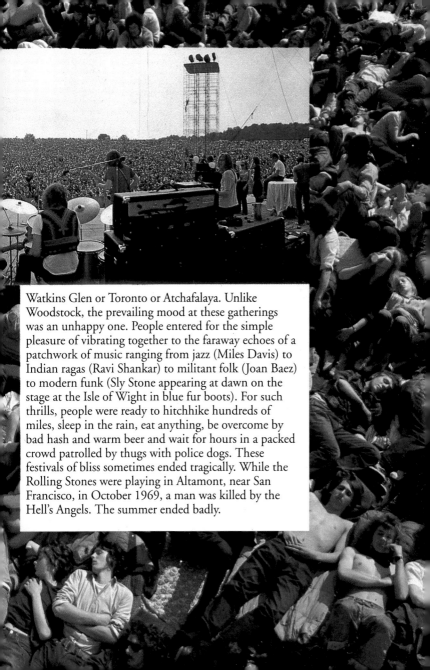

Watkins Glen or Toronto or Atchafalaya. Unlike
Woodstock, the prevailing mood at these gatherings
was an unhappy one. People entered for the simple
pleasure of vibrating together to the faraway echoes of a
patchwork of music ranging from jazz (Miles Davis) to
Indian ragas (Ravi Shankar) to militant folk (Joan Baez)
to modern funk (Sly Stone appearing at dawn on the
stage at the Isle of Wight in blue fur boots). For such
thrills, people were ready to hitchhike hundreds of
miles, sleep in the rain, eat anything, be overcome by
bad hash and warm beer and wait for hours in a packed
crowd patrolled by thugs with police dogs. These
festivals of bliss sometimes ended tragically. While the
Rolling Stones were playing in Altamont, near San
Francisco, in October 1969, a man was killed by the
Hell's Angels. The summer ended badly.

French business

Was nothing going on in Paris that summer of 1969? While the United States and Britain knew joyous musical upheavals, Paris contented itself with rumours and copies so pale they bordered on caricature. Very few French artists, in fact, understood the reach of pop culture in the sixties. Ronnie Bird reflected the mod spirit of London in 1965. Serge Gainsbourg made himself an amused commentator. Nino Ferrer tried to be inspired by the Stax sound in imitative songs. Some clubs opened up to English rock, but on the whole, France remained far behind.

Then came May 1968, with its student protests. Suddenly French students could no longer stand just to hear about 'swinging' London and 'druggy' California – they wanted the same things in Paris.

Rock and roll, the favoured means of expression, was one of the first beneficiaries of this awakening. Turning its back on Anglo-Saxon models, French pop music searched for new roots in folk music (Alan Stivell) or in several wild 'revolutionary' groups (Komintern, Red Noise).

But everything fell apart, and in five years pop's destruction of French rock and roll reduced to almost nothing the ferment from which had risen a legion of musicians. The absence of music classes and instrumental practice in the schools no longer favoured the development of talent. As a consequence, the only musicians to survive the aftermath of May 1968 in France were those highly influenced by jazz.

Pop music triumphs

Internationally, excess affected every level of production. There were record-breaking crowds at concerts (150,000 people for a Led Zeppelin concert) and record-breaking album sales. New records of notoriety, through the use of hype. New records of destruction of hotel rooms (the Who, Led Zeppelin). New records for the ingestion of various substances, which would cause the death of several heroes (Brian

In May 1968 Paris erupted with student protests. When the students took to the streets, shock troops were sent to gas and beat them. One outcome of this insurrection was the organization of a French concert and distribution network, all in the service of rock.

Jones in 1969, Jimi Hendrix and Janis
Joplin in 1970, Jim Morrison in 1971).
Always more, more, more.

With the arrival of hard rock at the
end of the sixties, the record for volume
also fell. By the end of 1968 Blue Cheer
had a hit with Eddie Cochran's 'Summertime Blues',
and MC5 *(Kick Out the Jams)* and Iggy Pop and the
Stooges *(The Stooges)* simply gave a more resonant
weight – in volume as well as in density – to the
patterns inherited from blues and rockabilly.

Led Zeppelin ('Stairway to Heaven') in Britain
continued the path traced by the Yardbirds: a hardened
blues sound with a heavy beat, embellished by
the virtuosity of its leader and guitarist, Jimmy
Page. The term 'heavy metal' appeared to designate
a radical approach. Blues-rock at the beginning, the
music then tended more and more to favour the
effect of density and volume, climaxing with the
painful (for the eardrums) absurdity of Grand
Funk Railroad.

In the United States, however, the meeting of urban
hard rock with southern blues generated the blossoming

L ed Zeppelin (above
Robert Plant and
the guitarist Jimmy Page)
could be considered the
first heavy metal group.
Initially inspired by
American blues
musicians, Jimmy Page
created a very complex
sonic universe. In
him the myth of the
'guitar hero' found its
full measure.

of groups like the Marshall Tucker Band *(A New Life)*, the Outlaws *(Lady in Waiting)*, Lynyrd Skynyrd ('Free Bird') and, above all, the Allman Brothers Band *(The Allman Brothers Band)*. The guitar playing of its leader, Duane Allman, who died in a 1971 motorcycle accident, influenced a number of artists, particularly his colleague Eric Clapton on 'Layla'. Further south, the Texas group ZZ Top ('Gimme All Your Lovin') offered a heavier, strongly rhythmic approach to the blues. The tradition was inherited from various musicians on the Houston scene, including Lightnin' Hopkins, and was continued by flamboyant guitarists from Johnny Winter to Stevie Ray Vaughan.

James Osterberg, called Iggy Pop (below left and right), incarnated the radical and violent rock of Detroit. With the Stooges (a name taken from the Three Stooges) he disturbed late-sixties America, reminding it that the ghettos were burning and that its youth had no future.

The aftermath of Woodstock

In California the stars of the sixties realigned themselves into supergroups like Crosby, Stills & Nash, who were joined later by Neil Young *(Harvest)*. In their wake a 'southern California' style appeared, reinforcing the myth forged by the Beach Boys. These records featured a laid-back atmosphere, polished production and a return to folk inspiration blended with good old country music. It was a 100-per cent American genre, occasionally fired up by songs bordering on parochialism (the Eagles'

1976 hit 'Hotel California'). Even Dylan rediscovered country and performed with Johnny Cash (*Nashville Skyline*, 1969). After the psychedelic storm, America searched for its roots and found them in Nashville.

In perfect harmony with the southern California rock trend, poetic and introspective songs regained a large audience. Even if they did not use the rhythm or the firepower of rock and roll, certain singer-songwriters belonged to this world in the late sixties and early seventies. It was a question of attitudes, references and associations. Leonard Cohen *(Songs from a Room)* and Joni Mitchell *(Blue)*, Tim Buckley *(Greetings from L.A.)* and Paul Simon *(There Goes Rhymin' Simon)*, Tom Waits *(Nighthawks at the Diner)* and James Taylor *(Sweet Baby James)* – regardless of their differences, their approaches and their singing styles – were recognized by the public as being part of the same family. An identical movement developed in Britain involving musicians searching for their roots in Celtic tradition – the Incredible String Band *(The 5000 Spirits or the Layers of the Onion)*, Fairport Convention *(Unhalfbricking)* and Pentangle *(Basket of Light)*.

Irritated by what they considered the general softening of music, disgusted by the blaring sounds of the triumphant progressive style (Supertramp, Emerson, Lake and Palmer, and their by-products), and indifferent to the exercise of virtuosity by jazz-rock musicians (the Mahavishnu Orchestra), lovers of true rock and roll worried about its survival.

The arrival of decadence

After the weak musical trends of the seventies, rock would regain its health, thanks to the proven remedies of outrage, provocation and surprise. The unexpected appearance of the group Sha Na Na at Woodstock foretold the future. Restlessly, rock looked for its

In 1973 no one expected the arrival of a group like the New York Dolls (above). The Dolls were a pure product of New York City's East Village, with their cheekiness, irreverence and appetite for provocation. Their capacity for playing vigorous, bracing and humorous rock and roll on just three chords inspired dozens of 'garage bands' – small groups from New York neighbourhoods. After the Dolls' premature break-up in 1975, their guitarist Johnny Thunders (opposite left and right) carried the flame of a tattered dandyism.

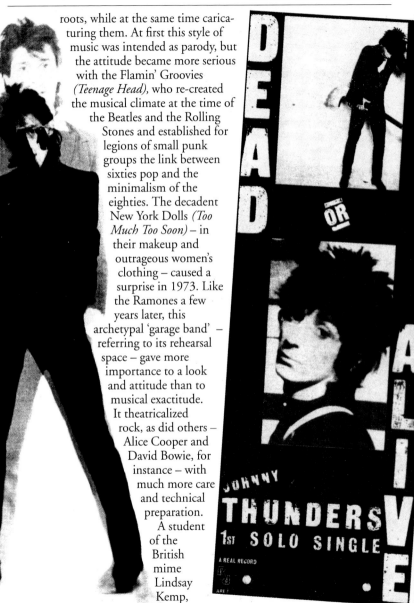

roots, while at the same time carica-
turing them. At first this style of
music was intended as parody, but
the attitude became more serious
with the Flamin' Groovies
(Teenage Head), who re-created
the musical climate at the time of
the Beatles and the Rolling
Stones and established for
legions of small punk
groups the link between
sixties pop and the
minimalism of the
eighties. The decadent
New York Dolls *(Too
Much Too Soon)* – in
their makeup and
outrageous women's
clothing – caused a
surprise in 1973. Like
the Ramones a few
years later, this
archetypal 'garage band' –
referring to its rehearsal
space – gave more
importance to a look
and attitude than to
musical exactitude.
It theatricalized
rock, as did others –
Alice Cooper and
David Bowie, for
instance – with
much more care
and technical
preparation.
A student
of the
British
mime
Lindsay
Kemp,

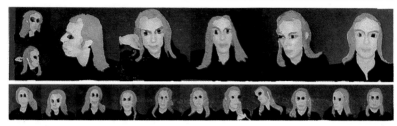

Bowie wanted to be an actor and singer. His carefully cultivated androgynous appearance shocked the world of rock used to the jeans of Californian musicians. Inevitably Bowie met Lou Reed, the other genius of provocation, and in 1972 Bowie produced Reed's album *Transformer*, which marked his great comeback after the Velvet Underground dissolved. Each in his own manner – Bowie's ode to Jean Genet and Reed's inventory of perversions at Andy Warhol's Factory – these two accomplices set the stage for a certain moral decay.

Seemingly more superficial, Bryan Ferry also played this game of affected decadence. After years of refusing the 'look', he rediscovered the pleasure of sequined costumes and stage makeup when he played with Roxy Music *(For Your Pleasure)*. Working close to Ferry for a short time was Brian Eno, who asserted himself as a dandy of the electronic age. His time with Roxy Music marked the appearance of the synthesizer in rock. Even he admitted that he was no musician, but he was a lover of experiments of all kinds, playing solo or in the company of other sound pioneers like Robert Fripp, Harold Budd and, later, David Byrne. He would also work as a producer and was associated with Bowie, Kraftwerk and U2, among others.

Just as extravagant but clearly more classical in their musical approach, Elton John *(Don't Shoot Me, I'm Only the Piano Player)* and Marc Bolan of the band T. Rex *(Electric Warrior)* conferred a sort of panache on the glam-rock of the seventies. At that time theatrical rock productions were all the rage, as magnificently illustrated by Genesis *(Selling England by the Pound)*, with Peter Gabriel and his numerous elaborate costumes.

From the first recordings of Roxy Music in 1972 to his later work without the band, Brian Eno (above) displayed remarkable command of the synthesizer, and his avant-garde experiments added another dimension to rock. His 1974 collaboration with guitarist Robert Fripp, like his later instrumental albums, was typical of a musical approach that could fit comfortably in the classical category.

Lou Reed (opposite centre) and David Bowie (opposite below) were the two principal heroes of seventies glam-rock, described by John Lennon as 'just rock and roll with lipstick on'. They shared an innate sense of theatricality, understanding how simultaneously to shock and seduce their audience. Their collaboration was sometimes stormy, even though it produced a masterpiece like Reed's 1972 album *Transformer*.

By the middle of the seventies, rock had become too complex, too removed from its original beat, too convoluted. The packaging had become more important than the contents. In the face of excessively slick and expensive productions, small groups had no chance to find their place in the sun. Pushed by the need to revive itself and rediscover its directness, rock sought refuge in the back of pubs. Once again the British scene came alive.

CHAPTER 6
NO FUTURE?

British punk rockers (left) aggressively expressed their refusal of a society that offered them no prospects. Their slogan became 'No future'.

In 1975 it was possible to hear a band practically every night in London for the price of a beer at the bar. Music made a grand return to the wholesome values of rhythm and blues in the hands of groups like Ducks Deluxe *(Ducks Deluxe)*, Dr Feelgood *(Private Practice)*, and Brinsley Schwarz *(Silver Pistol)*.

It did not take long for the excitement that reigned in the clubs to affect other spheres of musical production. Faced with the ill will of the big record companies towards newcomers, new groups sought refuge in independent labels as a way of recording and promoting their work. Virgin Records made a fortune in 1973 with the synthesizer hit *Tubular Bells* by Mike Oldfield, discovered Kevin Coyne and his warped blues and resurrected Robert Wyatt, thanks to his wonderful *Rock Bottom*. More centred on pub rock, in 1976–7 Stiff Records brought together several angry young men such as producer/performer Nick Lowe, Elvis Costello and Ian Dury, who, with his famous song 'Sex 'n' Drugs 'n' Rock 'n' Roll', would be caught up in the punk explosion.

A computer operator in a cosmetics company, Declan MacManus – alias Elvis Costello – did not have to modify his appearance much to resemble Buddy Holly. With his fighting stance and nasty stare, he tried in 1976 to reintroduce the aesthetic values of the fifties back into rock.

The birth of punk

The word *punk* used to refer to a marginal person, a naïf, a victim of the adult world. In 1967 Frank Zappa used the term in reference to the hippies of San Francisco. At the beginning of the seventies, rock critic Lester Bangs invented the description 'punk rock', which he associated with the 'B' groups assembled by Lenny Kaye for the important double album compilation *Nuggets*. For many years these garage bands were the training grounds for the cream of American rock: brilliant soloists including Todd Rundgren (Nazz),

In the late seventies, Ian Dury (below) incarnated the spirit of pub rock, music based on rhythm and blues played against a background of free-flowing taps and a convivial atmosphere.

Leslie West (the Vagrants and Mountain) and Ted Nugent (the Amboy Dukes), as well as such marginal but influential legends as the Electric Prunes and the Thirteenth Floor Elevator.

THE VELVET UNDERGROUND

An incredible book. It will shock and amaze you. A documentary on the sexual corruption of our age, it is a **must** for every thinking adult.

BY **MICHAEL LEIGH**
INTRODUCTION BY LOUIS BERG, M.D.

In the United States the punk scene spread out from CBGB, a club in New York City's East Village. At the end of its long, dark, narrow room, local garage bands ground out a primitive, aggressive rock. The Velvet Underground, with its Warholian spirit, constituted one of the only two admissible reference points; the other, strangely enough, was French poetry: Patti Smith *(Horses)* and Richard Hell (and the Voidoids, *Blank Generation*) quoted

Rock and roll searched for references in cinema, literature and the fine arts. The Velvet Underground took its name from a novel on sado-masochism (left) as a bohemian spirit wafted over the East Village of New York.

Rimbaud, and Tom Miller called himself Tom Verlaine. Their music as well as their attitude reflected the neo-romanticism of a new Beat Generation, as it was dubbed by William Burroughs. Knowing they would lose from the start, they refused all hit-parade ambitions, taking on a nihilistic, often self-destructive, attitude. Some would die, victims of drug overdoses. During this short period in the late seventies, rock again found its intensity, its flashes of craziness and its urgency in the work, for example, of the Ramones, Blondie and the Talking Heads.

CBGB's example would soon spill across America. Punk groups sprang up from the streets of Cleveland (the Dead Boys), Boston (the Modern Lovers), Los Angeles (X), and even San Francisco (the Dead Kennedys). Directly descended from the Velvet Underground, the Stooges, the Heartbreakers and MC5, this explosion of urban rock was, among other things, a response to the general tendency on FM radio of playing dull pop music.

The exception to this trend was Bruce Springsteen, who succeeded by operating on an

dead boys

FRI AUG 22

CENTRO SOCIA
609 LINCOLN ST S
Tickets available at MIRACLE MUSIC, Stock

Punk rock took hold of New York at CBGB in the East Village.

The Dead Kennedys along with Black Flag (posters above and below) represented the punk wave on the West Coast.

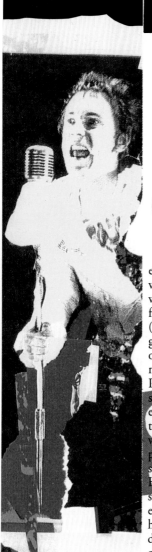

NEVER MIND THE BOLL OCKS

HERE'S THE

entirely different
wavelength. The son of a
working-class New Jersey
family, Springsteen
(nicknamed 'The Boss')
grew up on the outskirts
of New York in the no-
man's-land of Asbury
Park. He retained the
simple charm of an
everyman, easily winning
the hearts of the crowds
who came to hear him
play from the mid-
seventies *(Born to Run)*.
His rhythm-and-blues–
soaked music, his
emotional singing style,
his lyrics recounting the
daily life of the working
class – halfway between
social commentary and

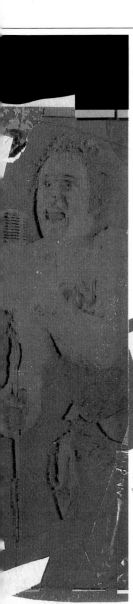

moral tale – and his ability to identify with a generation seeking justice and pride *(The River)* conferred on him a stature equal to Bob Dylan's ten years earlier. The comparison was unavoidable, though Springsteen never concerned himself with spirituality.

Springsteen led a 'blue collar' movement that would include Bob Seger, Huey Lewis and Southside Johnny (also from New Jersey), who reacted to an urban mechanized society in a virile way, sticking close to the roots of rhythm and blues. Through the years this style has become emblematic of American rock.

Britain discovers punks

In 1975 Malcolm McLaren split his time between managing the New York Dolls, at the end of their career, and running his boutique on King's Road in London. He was motivated by the little-known but highly influential sixties philosophy of situationism (which saw art as action and cultural critique) and, like many others, grew tired of the greediness of show business and the new rock stars' mania for power. He wanted to launch a new group that would satisfy his taste for provocation and at the same time rediscover the raw energy and outrageousness of the pioneers of rock. In 1976 the Sex Pistols would personify his

John Lydon – alias Johnny Rotten (opposite) – was the leader of the Sex Pistols. His extraordinary stage presence threw the other musicians into the shadows. The only exception was the bassist, Sid Vicious, who succeeded in making a name for himself at the cost of self-destruction: he lacerated his chest with shards of glass, physically attacked the audience, was beaten up in return, swallowed all sorts of drugs, killed his girlfriend in a New York hotel and finished by dying of an overdose in 1979. In two short years (1976–8) the Sex Pistols had succeeded in turning rock upside down and in bringing some of its fundamental values – outrage, theatricalized violence, defiance of the established order and objection to the ideals offered up by their own culture – back into fashion. More than fifteen years later the punk-rock stimulus still disturbs and continues to make converts.

ANARCHY IN THE U.K.

desires *(Never Mind the Bollocks Here's the Sex Pistols)*.

What did it matter if Johnny Rotten and Sid Vicious could barely recognize a note of music? Shoplifters (found in McLaren's store!), riffraff, junkies, vandals, they were chosen because they looked like small-time thugs. Representing a marginal scene adopted by the media, they were the perfect antidote to the jubilee celebrations for the Queen in 1977. A powerful trend developed, characterized in particular by self-destruction: pallid faces, torn clothes, pierced skin, shaved heads or hair glued into multicoloured Mohawk crests. English punk turned its back on the elegance of such princes of pop as Elton John. Designers Vivienne Westwood (McLaren's partner at the time) and Bernie Rhodes (manager of the Clash) transported the punk look into the world of fashion.

While the Sex Pistols were recording the reign of anarchy in Britain, the Clash (opposite) preached armed revolt. Joe Strummer (below right) was in part its brain, its 'theorist'. His group expressed the frustration of youth faced with a future of unemployment and police harassment in cities stricken by economic crisis. Through its songs and adoption of reggae protest tunes, the Clash also expressed solidarity with Jamaican immigrants in Britain.

Spirited and politicized, the Clash *(The Clash)* came on the scene in 1976 and were followed by hundreds of groups (like X-Ray Spex and Sham '69) who rediscovered rebellion, that fundamental quality of rock and roll. Even with little means and limited

knowledge of music, each could get on stage, and the Roxy Club in London saw a long line of bands influenced by both the sixties and the punks: the Jam *(In the City)*, the Buzzcocks *(Another Music in a Different Kitchen)*, the Damned *(Damned, Damned, Damned)* and the Gang of Four *(Entertainment)*. Small labels such as Radar, Rough Trade and Sire flourished. But for this generation hit by economic crisis, the dismal observation of 'no future' was the only response – quite a contrast to the positive and open ideas of the Woodstock generation.

The new wave

In 1978 the public wavered between the raw energy of punk nihilism and the ethereal, elegant, sophisticated music offered them at the same time by two new bands, the Police *(Outlandos d'Amour)* and Dire Straits ('Sultans of Swing'). Like Eric Clapton earlier on, the Police were influenced by Jamaican reggae as symbolized by Bob Marley, while Dire Straits explored a vein closer to the relaxed southern rock practised by J. J. Cale. Their almost immediate worldwide success reached several generations of listeners.

The recurrent tendency of rock to search for support from the largest crowd – obvious for simple commercial reasons – ended up creating concerts in gigantic stadiums where stars like Madonna flaunted themselves. Hypnotized, the media paid little attention to the fact that such artists obscured the intense wave of creativity

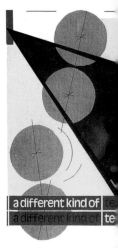

The Buzzcocks of Manchester recalled the Small Faces band of the mod era: ordinary kids in appearance, amphetamine-addicted rockers in reality. This sixties reference was not uncommon in the British new wave in 1977, as can be seen in the work of another group, the Jam.

that punk and new wave were producing in unexpected places.

When Ian Curtis killed himself in Manchester in 1980, his band, Joy Division *(Unknown Pleasures)*, was already the obligatory touchstone for the new wave movement. His music translated the gloominess of the modern world into an intense, emotion-charged atmosphere. The Cure, London suburbanites clearly haunted by the shadow of the poet Shelley, also laid claim to a sombre romanticism. Sardonic, disillusioned offspring of the first punks, these groups contrasted sharply with the mainstream tendencies of the eighties: clear ambition and artificiality, with much more attention paid to cultivating a look than a musical signature (Duran Duran, Spandau Ballet).

In between, the arrival of the music video, largely broadcast by specialized cable channels like MTV, focused on physical appearance and stage settings. Musicians who were older – or less 'cute' – were penalized, regardless of their talent. Some, like the fine British rhythm and blues musician Joe Jackson, rebelled against this conformity and the censorship in effect on

Robert Smith formed the Cure in 1978 in the London suburbs. One of the band's first songs, 'Killing an Arab', was inspired by Albert Camus' *The Stranger*. These sombre romanticists had numerous imitators who copied their attitudes, their clothes and their hair.

The Irish group U2 (left) incarnated certain national values: passion, openness, idealism. Everything seemed to indicate that the term 'heroic' was invented just to describe U2. The group received top billing at large charity concerts, on the same level as Sting, Peter Gabriel and Bruce Springsteen. These artists brought a needed measure of soul back to rock and roll after years of indifference, frenzied ambition and cynicism – indeed, of pure and simple nihilism.

television. Others shrewdly appealed to video and cinema to pass across their message. Thus, for example, Michael Jackson entrusted the creation of a short film for his 1982 song 'Thriller' to Hollywood director John Landis. Without a doubt the film's success played a large role in the high level of record sales.

At the same time as the rock video, the compact disc turned the music business upside down. The successful reissues of back catalogue material reinvigorated overlooked groups and movements. Suddenly, rock turned its attention to the past, recycling it, not inventing much that was new. Obsessed with profits, the huge machinery of the music business wore out. Events such as Live Aid, organized by Bob Geldof in 1985, helped to ease social conscience and focused world attention on the famine in Africa.

World rock

But rock endures. Throughout its history, whenever inspiration was missing, people looked to old successful favourites. The Rolling Stones had adapted Chuck Berry and were copied in their turn by the Black Crowes, Telephone and dozens of garage bands.

Today, the range of influence has drastically enlarged. Starting in 1965, when George Harrison brought the sitar to the music of the Beatles, musicians have learned to delve into popular music the world over. That search has conferred on rock a kind of new 'world' dimension, as is clear in the work of musicians as far apart as Peter Gabriel, David Byrne and Paul Simon.

Rock is in good shape, regardless of those who relentlessly predict its demise. Small labels are thriving and with them the hundreds of groups who are returning to the simple values of guitars connected to electricity. The politically conscious

song has rediscovered its vigour and its audience through Tracy Chapman ('Fast Cars') and Sinéad O'Connor (*I Do Not Want What I Haven't Got*) and urban rappers. Current events offer a bottomless supply of issues to protest. After the disappearance of disco music, so popular in the seventies, dance has recovered its place in 'rave parties', spontaneous gatherings around a booming bass

sound. And now, after Memphis, Liverpool and Manchester, there is a new focus: Seattle, with its 'grunge' movement (Nirvana, *Nevermind*). Periodically victim of its own megalomania, rock always manages to rebound, drawing new strength from the inexhaustible reservoir of its audience. Elvis Presley can sleep peacefully. There'll be 'Good Rockin' Tonight'.

Rock has always been fascinated by new technology, risking the loss of its simplicity, warmth and effectiveness. The icy synthesizers of the seventies and eighties happily gave way to the 'samplers' (snippets of sound) of house music. Dance became an essential element again. Rap, funk and its electronic cousin, techno-funk, enlivened 'rave parties', improvised gatherings focused around a huge sound system and a disc jockey skilled at linking rhythms. The majority of these musical styles originated in the inner cities of America. All the rules were turned upside down, the music business exploded and everyone managed to produce and distribute their music outside the traditional circuits.

Left: illustration from a Kinks album cover.

Overleaf: Keith Richards of the Rolling Stones.

DOCUMENTS

Supergroups, megastars and giant
festivals – the world of rock expresses
itself in superlatives.

Frankly speaking

When you give rockers the floor, they don't mince words. Those who are not specifically interested in promoting their latest album take the time to cast on their craft – and sometimes their colleagues – an eye as critical, frank and direct as their music. It was not too long ago that the Beatles caused an uproar by stating that they were more popular than Jesus Christ. Insolence is also a fundamental quality of rock and roll.

The truth about rock and roll

Has rock and roll become too self-indulgent?

No, I didn't say that. It is the interpretation that is too self-indulgent. We're led to believe that the music that was in fact simple and direct at the beginning was actually really complex and difficult. You can blame that on business, on the greed of some people, on the star system. There's an enormous gap between what things are and the way people perceive them.

People like me don't have a firm opinion on anything. I am just as stupid as the average guy. They pretend that I say things, but basically I do my job like everyone else. I write songs. Everyone knows more or less how that's done, OK? But

Iggy Pop.

they created this concept in the sixties.… I have been confined to this role, I have been pushed into this box for business reasons. However, the concept is false, completely false. But since nothing else exists, I do my best to live with it.

Van Morrison
Les Inrockuptibles, August 1989

Rock and roll out of jail

What did your parents think at the time of the first Stooges albums?
I think they were terrified, but they are very nice people who have never prevented me from doing what I wanted.

Oh, yes, one time, my father was really angry. We gave a concert in the city where he taught. I broke a bottle against my microphone stand and the glass flew in every direction. A shard cut a girl in the first row on the arm.… I had to get out of there quickly because the audience was going to lynch me. Later on, the cops nabbed me and brought me to the station. The next day, a local newspaper printed the court minutes of the incident. And everybody saw it, my parents' friends, my father – in short, the whole world. They held that against me. But he was a really good father. He got me out of jail when I was younger. He even came to my concerts.

Iggy Pop
Les Inrockuptibles
June 1990

The sex machine rolls on

'God got me in on the ground floor of every kind of music,' [James] Brown exults backstage at Radio City Music Hall. 'He put me into the game before Prince and Sly and Rick James and the Funkadelics. When – '

Instantly Brown cancels the thought and explodes with a torrential verbal outburst: 'SEXMACHINEGOOD FOOTTHINKDOINGITTODEATH ICAN'TSTANDMYSELFWHEN YOUTOUCHMESUPERBAD COLDSWEATFUNKYCHICKEN INEEDYOURLOVESOBADBABY BABYBABY!'

He pauses, grinning ferociously, and spews it out again. The feat of precisely merged enunciation is doubly impressive on the second pass, the humming whole too specific to be psychobabble or doggerel filler, and yet not exactly a boast either. It's more of an involuntary mantra disclosure.

'Down in D.C. they talking about the go-go but I had them kids out in the streets while they were still babies, doing the popcorn with the Original Disco Man. Funk I invented back in the fifties. The rap thing I had down on my "Brother Rapp (Part I)", and you can check that. I enjoyed my thing with Afrika Bambaataa on "Unity", but I did it more for the message than for the music. Michael Jackson, he used to watch me from the wings and got his moon walk from my camel walk – he'll tell you that if you ask. Same way, I was slippin' and slidin' before Prince was out of his crib; that's why Alan Leeds, who used to work for my organization, is on his management team, tipping and hipping him. I ain't jealous, I'm zealous. I ain't teased, I'm *pleased.* Who's gonna do James Brown better'n *James Brown?* Think!'

Timothy White
Rock Lives, 1990

Rock and roll: too much

It is totally a prisoner of its reputation and its myth. For me, life is much simpler if one forgets rock and roll a little. I draw the line there. I prefer that one speak of 'Lou Reed music' as my subject. That way, there are no limits, no prohibitions, no 'you can't do that', none of that blah-blah…. No one dares say that about a novel or a film, but as soon as the subject is a rock and roll record, everything is permitted.

Let's stop this imposture then…. Rock and roll is irrelevant.

Is rock and roll totally empty now?
All these definitions, they wear me out. Rock and roll is much too restrained for me. I don't like to feel enclosed. I write lyrics an adult can identify with. My new album, *Magic & Loss,* doesn't mean a thing to a kid. I don't write for kids. I haven't written for that audience since 1976. I always wanted to escape from the futility of rock lyrics. If I write, it is for adults to amuse themselves with a little bit of rock and roll, while listening to lyrics that engage them mentally.

Lou Reed
Les Inrockuptibles, January 1992

Lou Reed.

Ice-T thaws out

The rapper muses on past controversies.

RJ SMITH: You go out of your way in interviews to say that you regret things you've said in the past about gay people. I wonder why you do that.
ICE-T: You know, you just grow up. Not just about gay people but about life. When you come from the kind of neighborhood I grew up in, masculinity is at a premium. The jungle creed says

the strong must feed on any prey at hand. That's just how it is. So everybody who is weaker than you, you say, 'You're a faggot, sissy.' It's not even based so much on sexuality, it's something on weakness. You looked on as weak. At some point, you say, 'I thought being gay was something you choose to be.' After further analysis, I feel that some people don't make a choice, it's a way they probably are born. You grow up and you learn, you don't just *know*. It's hard for someone who's brought up in a very masculine arena called the ghetto – it is an arena, you are thrown into this pit. Even people who aren't tough learn to walk tough.

I used to say things at our concerts

that were stupid. Like we'd say, 'Everybody with AIDS be quiet.' We didn't know what AIDS *was*. AIDS is serious. You die. I'm not beyond saying, yo, I'm wrong. But you gotta understand that everybody does not grow up in the same way.

My whole thing is: I'm straight. I don't even dig the use of the word *straight* because that says that somebody else is crooked. But I still don't totally understand it. Men kissing – I just don't totally understand it. But I think that's a little too much for you to ask of me. The same way that you might not be able to come into touch with some of the anger I have for the system. But I leave it at that. I ain't got anything to say about anybody gay. If that's your thing, cool.

RJ SMITH: Do you regret printing the lyrics to 'Cop Killer' in the liner notes?

ICE-T: Well, in the new album we didn't put 'em in there. After you see your lyrics blown up 30 feet tall.… I know they can still transcribe the lyrics off the vocals, 'cause I rap real legibly, but I didn't print them on *Home Invasion* as a way of letting people feel censorship. Maybe one day we might have to have records where they come with a special decoder that will bring out the lyrics.

In a way, when we pulled 'Cop Killer' it was a form of censorship. It's kind of good now, 'cause people come up and say, 'Can I still get a copy?' And I'm like, 'Nope'. That's what censorship is like. It's a way of hitting you in the face when you can't buy it. Now the ones on the streets are turning into collector's items.

RJ SMITH: How much does 'Cop Killer' sell for now?

ICE-T: They were selling it up in Santa Barbara for $300 if it's still sealed.

RJ SMITH: What about fans who say you're Ice-T and you're not supposed to back down to anybody?

ICE-T: I got to call my own shots. And they don't really know when it's a back down or when it's a retreat to return with superior firepower. You never know. You might say, 'Oh, Ice-T backed down.' But what good is me holding that record out there when I can't hit with another record? Warner Bros. wasn't going to back me on *Cop Killer 2* or *The Return of the Cop Killer*.

It wasn't really a form of weakness.

RJ Smith
'T-ing Off: This Time It's Personal'
The Village Voice, 13 April 1993

Enya expresses herself

The Irish singer's international hit 'Orinoco Flow', on Watermark *helped make her name as a soloist.*

Anything other than music is irrelevant to me. It is not that I am shielding myself or guarding myself.… I have no boyfriends, no hobby. Everything has had to be put aside while I have worked on my music. I believe you have only one chance to make a life and to do your work. That I have put first. That is why there is *Watermark*.… Almost all the music is played by me. It is recorded in real time. This is how we keep the music human. When we will perform live … a real choir will sing with me as I play my instruments. This is my tradition. And I sing many songs in Irish because Irish is the language of my home and my friends. It is a language that expresses feeling much more directly than English.

Jim Fouratt
'Above the Watermark'
Spin magazine, May 1989

Eric Clapton: reluctant god

The ... burden he clearly wanted to rid himself of was the reluctant role of guitar god; he was more than ready to abdicate in favour of Jimi Hendrix. 'I'm very surprised I've got a reputation,' he said with unnecessary self-deprecation. 'You assume people have forgotten you, then you get a super show and get surprised at how much people expect of you. I do worry a lot about this. I don't know if my playing keeps up with my image. I do my best. I'm happy if I've got a little riff to play. I don't see myself as a great solo guitarist – that's not my bag, that's Jimi's.... I'm very aware of the pressures of reputation and image and it's all bullshit. I think I'm good enough, which is true and false. I can only do my best.'

John Pidgeon
Eric Clapton: A Biography, 1985

Sting on the problems of success

Those pressures of wealth and fame that were piling up on you, were they very difficult to come to terms with?
I have to say that I was enjoying success at the same time as it was a nightmare. It's a double-edged thing. It's nice to make a lot of money, but it also brings a lot of problems with it. You know, what do you do with it? Where do you put it? Do you deserve it? What about all the poor people in the world? All of these things, that if you're a thinking person, you have to deal with, and we were asked to deal with it over a very short period of time. We went from being church mice to being wealthy, and I know I sound like I'm giving myself a hard time, but it's not easy. A lot of people would say, 'I'd love that problem.' (LAUGHS) I'm

sure they would. But when you're in the public eye, it's difficult. I'm glad I've got money, but when you first get it it's a problem. That's why a lot of rock stars lose it immediately. It's a combination of incompetence and guilt. I still have mine.

John Pidgeon
Classic Albums: Interviews from the Radio One Series, 1991

Mick Hucknall of Simply Red

'I can't get fucked up like I used to, I'm too fit. I drink a bit of wine but I don't drink anything else really. I don't hit the top shelf.' Nevertheless he is at pains to point out a reformed streak in his character: 'When you come off the road then you realize that the world doesn't revolve around you. When you're on tour everything's done for you, everything. They tell you when to go to bed, when to get up, what time to eat, when the show is. Then you come out of it and you call a friend and say, I wanna see you, come round, and they say, I can't, I'm working. You think, You always used to see me, but yeah, they always saw you on your terms. So then I had to start being a little bit more understanding and see that other people have got their lives and I have to wait and I have got to learn to wait and that was a great instruction for me.'

Clearly worried that he may be painting a portrait of 'a really nice guy', Hucknall recovers his composure: 'The press have to have a new angle every time there's a new album, You're off the drugs, or You've found God, or You've found something. Well, I haven't found anything: I'm just having a great time.'

Interview by John Naughton
Q, October 1991

U2 on the verge of fame in 1980

'London is supposed to be permissive. London is supposed to be freedom! London is traps. London is boxes. London is chained in bondage, in fact. And if a band coming from Thick Paddy Land – and that is not true – comes along and tells these people what's up they might not be awfully pleased.'

A number of times during my weekend visit to Ireland, Bono hints that a move to London is all but inevitable. The type of move they (reluctantly) want to make is somewhere between the decision of The Undertones to leave Derry and to tour constantly but always return, and The Boomtown Rats, who have now disowned the fatherland.

'Everyone from the Rats has left the country really bitter,' explained Bono. 'I won't leave this country bitter at all. The plan is that if we have to leave, and we're still not sure, it will only be for a while. It's basically that we feel the group has to be thrown into different circumstances if it's going to be stimulated, if it's going to change. It would be very easy to stay here. But we'll go ... and we have to come back.'

Bono of U2
Interview by Paul Morley in 1980
New Musical Express, 16 March 1991

George Michael on sexuality

I don't think there's anything wrong in marketing yourself sexually at all. People are sometimes uncomfortable when they see men doing it, but part of what makes certain men stars is the way they promote themselves in the manner that women do all the time. Women are allowed to project sexuality as part of their personalities; it's seen as something beautiful. If a guy does it, on a day to day level, there's normally a 'medallion-man' type of reaction, but up on screen it's more acceptable. If you do it well, do it with a certain conviction, I think it can be very appealing. In my case, people don't seem to have found it a turn off.

Interview by Alan Jackson
New Musical Express, 20 June 1987

The Pet Shop Boys: rock versus disco

'Having said that,' Neil [Tennant] concedes, 'when people say disco music has crap lyrics ... it does. But *rock* music has crap lyrics, and the idea of the Pet Shop Boys was to have disco music with introspective lyrics, political lyrics....

'Most people in the rock business are incredibly limited. They either think oh yeah, disco crap, or they kind of *patronizingly* like Rick Astley's record 'cos it's ... *fun*.... But disco music is the most advanced form of popular music, in terms of progression, that there is. All disco music advances the genre of dance music, of *popular music*. Rock music doesn't! What's *rock music* ever done since ... Jimi Hendrix, maybe? Every rock group, every pop group is influenced by hip-hop, Hi Energy, house.... It's the genre that gave you the 12" single, it's the genre that gave you the entire technological revolution that's happened in the last 10 years. None of it's rock music! It's all dance music! To the extent that every rock group has a 12" record now. And now every disco group has a rock record.'

Interview by David Quantick
New Musical Express, 15 October 1988

John Lennon and the Beatles

In 1973 John Lennon looked back on the phenomenon known as the Beatles. But he also had something to say about the present day.

Always the Beatles were talked about and the Beatles talked about themselves as being four parts of the same person....
What's happened to those four parts?
They remembered that they were four individuals. You see we believed the Beatles myth, too. I don't know whether the others still believe it. We were four guys.... I met Paul and said 'You want to join me band?' you know. Then George joined and then Ringo joined. We were just a band who made it very, very big, that's all. Our best work was never recorded.

Why?
Because we were performers ... in Liverpool, Hamburg and other dance halls and what we generated was fantastic, where we played straight rock, and there was nobody to touch us in Britain. As soon as we made it, we made it, but the edges were knocked off. [Manager] Brian [Epstein] put us in suits and all that and we made it very, very big. But we sold out, you know. The music was dead before we even went on the theatre tour of Britain....

How would you trace the breakup of the Beatles?
After Brian died we collapsed. Paul took over and supposedly led us. But what is leading us when we went round in circles? We broke up then....

What was your feeling when Brian died?
The feeling that anybody has when somebody close to them dies. There is a sort of little hysterical, sort of hee, hee, I'm glad it's not me, or something in it,

John Lennon. Right: the Fab Four.

you know? That funny feeling when somebody dies. I don't know whether you've had it, I've had a lot of people die on me. And the other feeling is What? What the f—! You know, what can I do? I knew that we were in trouble then. I didn't really have any misconceptions about our ability to do anything other than play music and I was scared. I thought, 'we've f—in' had it.'...

How did Paul react?
I don't know how the others took it. You can never tell ... it's no good asking me ... it's like asking me how you took it, you know, I don't know. I'm in me own head. I can't be in anybody else's. I don't know really what George, Paul or Ringo think any more than I do about, you

know. I know them pretty well, but I don't know anybody that well. Yoko I know about the best. I don't know how they felt. It was my own thing. We were all just dazed....

Do you think you're a genius?
Yes, if there is such a thing as one, I am one.

When did you first realize that?
When I was about twelve. I used to think I must be a genius but nobody's noticed. I used to think whether I'm a genius or I'm mad, which is it? I used to think, well, I can't be mad because nobody's put me away; therefore, I'm a genius. I mean genius is a form of madness and we're all that way. But I used to be a bit coy about it, you know, like me guitar playing, you know. If

there is such a thing as genius, which is just what … what the f— is it, I am one, you know, and if there isn't, I don't care. I used to think it when I was a kid, writing me poetry and doing me paintings. I didn't become something when the Beatles made it, or when you heard about me, I've been like this all me life. Genius is pain, too. It's just pain.…

What was it like, say, running around discotheques with the Stones?
… We were kings and we were all just at the prime and we all used to just go around London in our cars and meet each other and talk about music with the Animals and Eric [Burdon] and all that. It was really a good time. That was the best period, fame-wise, we didn't get mobbed so much. I don't know, it was like a men's smoking club, just a very good scene.…

And you feel the same way about rock and roll now at 30 as you did at 15?
Well, it will never be as new and it will never do what it did to me then, but like 'Tutti Frutti' or 'Long Tall Sally' is pretty avant-garde. I met an old avant-garde friend of Yoko's in the Village the other day who was talking about one note like he just discovered that. That's about as far out as you can get. Even intellectually I can play games enough for reasons why that music is very important and always will be. Like the blues, as opposed to jazz, white middle class good jazz as opposed to the blues … the blues is better.…

Because it's simpler?
Because it's real, it's not perverted or thought about, it's not a concept, it is a chair, not a design for a chair, or a better chair, or a bigger chair, or a chair with leather or with design … it is the first chair. It is a chair for sitting on, not chairs for looking at or being appreciated. You sit on that music.…

Are you the Beatles?
No, I'm not the Beatles. I'm me. Paul isn't the Beatles. Brian Epstein wasn't the Beatles, neither is Dick James. The Beatles are the Beatles. Separately, they are separate. George was a separate individual singer, with his own group as well, before he came in with us, the Rebel Rousers. Nobody is the Beatles. How could they be? We all had our roles to play … I don't believe in the Beatles.… I don't believe in them whatever they were supposed to be in everybody's head, including our own heads for a period. It was a dream. I don't believe in the dream anymore.…

Who do you think is good today? In any arts…
The unfortunate thing about ego-maniacs is that they don't take much attention of other people's work. I only assess people on whether they are a danger to me or my work or not.

Yoko is as important to me as Paul and Dylan rolled into one. I don't think she will get recognition until she's dead. There's me, and maybe I could count the people on one hand that have any conception of what she is or what her mind is like, or what her work means to this f—in' idiotic generation. She has the hope that she might be recognized. If I can't get recognized, and I'm doing it in a f—in' clown's costume, I'm doing it on the streets, you know, I don't know what – I admire Yoko's work.

I admire 'Fluxus', a New York-based group of artists founded by George

Beatles fans were like no other.

Macuinas. I really think what they do is beautiful and important.

I admire Andy Warhol's work, I admire Zappa a bit, but he's a f—in' intellectual – I can't think of anybody else. I admire people from the past. I admire Fellini. A few that Yoko's educated me to…. She's educated me into things that I didn't know about before, because of the scene I was in; I'm getting to know some other great work that's been going on now and in the past – there is all sorts going on.

I still love Little Richard, and I love Jerry Lee Lewis. They're like primitive painters….

Chuck Berry is one of the all-time great poets, a rock poet you could call him. He was well advanced of his time lyric-wise. We all owe a lot to him, including Dylan. I've loved everything he's done, ever. He was in a different class from the other performers, he was in the tradition of the great blues artists but he really wrote his own stuff – I know Richard did, but Berry *really* wrote stuff, just the lyrics were fantastic, even though we didn't know what he was saying half the time.

Jann Wenner
Lennon Remembers: The Rolling Stone Interviews, 1973

Some women rockers

Long confined to secondary roles – fans, groupies, backup singers – in the middle of the sixties female singers began to occupy centre stage. Janis Joplin immediately springs to mind. Hundreds of women rockers followed her example and have played the game as well as their male counterparts. Siouxsie, Patti Smith, Madonna and Annie Lennox owe her more than a little something.

Janis Joplin

Adored by hippies and Hell's Angels alike, Janis Joplin was a legend in her own time.

Janis' Lyon Street apartment had a quaintly curved balcony that soaked up the rays of the afternoon sun. In the front room of the flat, which cost all of seventy-five dollars a month, Linda Gravenites slept on a large, comfortable couch and, by the great natural light of the day, did all her sewing. A tiny kitchen jagged off to one side of a large entry hall and in the back was Janis' bedroom, all dark and draped with the emblems of seduction, the final enrichment to Janis' image. Velvet and satin swathed her bed; her windows were veiled with lace and silk. One wall stood clear of sensuous enticement, its attraction a series of posters, Janis portrayed by her photographer friend Bob Seidemann. There were animals, always essential to Janis' happiness. A romping half collie named George enhanced the charm of the apartment; an aloof cat named Sam stalked possessively about. There were friends and laughter and Linda. All in all, it was, or should have been, the best year of Janis' life.

Rehearsals occupied the days, performances her weekend nights. Most of all, she had attained acceptance. She had trimmed down to a slight and attractive figure. She had acquired an aura, which, while not of a conventional beauty, had the irresistible radiance of energy. No longer an outcast, at twenty-four she was a queen, and if the regal chamber of her bedroom saw no permanence, wasn't she too young for that anyway, and wasn't her lofty status the reason, and didn't a revolving but continual solace to her flesh cushion the wilderness of her heart a little – just a little? Besides, what the hell, it was just one jazzy trick after another.

One day, just like any other day, Janis took George for a walk through the Panhandle. Resting on the grass for a while, she broke her boredom by throwing a stick for the dog to chase and return to her feet. Tired of the game, she pulled herself up and continued through the park, then stopped as a familiar figure came sauntering over the grass.

'Man, haven't seen you in ages!' Janis smiled.

'Yeah, long time. How's it going?'

Janis shrugged, going on to chat about her music and a number of other matters. 'I need something new,' she sighed.

'What've you been doing?'

Oh, this and ... a little smack. I'm kind of strung out, though.'

'What's it like?' Janis asked. 'I've done it a couple of times, but I didn't like it, 'cause I always got really sick.'

'Yeah,' the girl nodded. 'Well, I got sick the first couple of times too.'

Janis peered at her curiously.

'The high's a groove, ya know ... but it's a drag to be strung out. Listen, I gotta meet somebody. See ya around, right?'

Janis waved as she turned around to walk back in the direction of her apartment. George dipped his head towards her feet and pranced happily behind her as she headed home.

Myra Friedman
Buried Alive: The Biography of Janis Joplin, 1973

Janis Joplin.

Siouxsie

Back in the good old days when she was a go-go dancer for The Pistols, Siouxsie twisted by the side of the stage decked out in her black leather peek-a-boo brassiere, swastika arm-band and fish-net pantaloons, until Malcolm [McLaren] decided to drop the Pan's Pistols schtick and poor S.S. – no chicken herself – was rendered redundant.

The S.S. girl found herself in the S. S. (Social Security) queue alongside another Rotten reject Sid Vicious (unemployed drummer), and on the rebound they formed a combo called Siouxsie and The Banshees with the help of two guitar-picking cronies.

Sid soon left to be replaced by another loser, but Siouxsie's songs –'Metal', 'Surburban Relapse', 'Helter Skelter' (rumour has it that Siouxsie is a Rutle Rocker), 'Carcass' and 'Love in A Void' (which contains the typical line 'Too many Jews for my liking') are still inspired by horror films, Charles Manson and nastiness in general to a back-drop of

chain-store beer-keller muzak.

Despite being a suburban mother-lover who still rooms with her silver-haired mater, Siouxsie does not let her love of family life interfere with the serious task of bread-winning, and The Banshees toured constantly for two years *après* punk, until Polydor took pity on them in the summer of 1978.

Julie Burchill and Tony Parsons
'The Boy Looked at Johnny', 1978

Punk bands

Sexual politics informed the most interesting 'inner-circle' punk groups. 'Punk became more macho as people's rock 'n' roll tendencies started to sneak back out again,' says Viv Albertine of the Slits, 'but there were those who stuck with questioning. The whole thing was about looking at things with a fresh eye, and sexuality had to be looked at, there were so many problems in there that had to be solved. And that meant stepping back. We all worked on each other's guitar, bass, singing, everything. It was painful, but we were very strict with each other.'

The difficulty for groups like the Slits and Siouxsie and the Banshees was how to translate an often obnoxious and proud attitude into a new form of music. No woman had made these noises before. For the Slits, the result was a maelstrom of over-amped guitar and sheet-metal drumming and, amid the chaos, musicians creating their own order. By the autumn, the 'armed playground chants' of songs like 'Love and Romance' and 'Vindictive' had become full-blown streetfights, anarchic and threatening.

Siouxsie and the Banshees played off Siouxsie's dominatrix-style hauteur against three pretty-boy musicians.

By the late autumn [1977], they were playing songs full of awkward twists, casual brutalities, mass-media trash and the intense excitement of ambition outstripping ability. 'We weren't musicians,' says Siouxsie, 'talking about breaking down walls and actually doing it are quite different things. In our naivety we started making this noise that was ours.'

Jon Savage
England's Dreaming, 1991

Patti Smith

You had heard of or read the name of Patti Smith here and there: She had published some short texts and record reviews (altogether rather banal) in *Creem* and *Rolling Stone.* Several collections of bizarrely fascinating poems appeared under her name: *Witt' Seventh Heaven,* with their references to Rimbaud, Brian Jones and Mickey Spillane. The words, made to be very loudly read, chanted, spit out, howled, struck you with their rhythm. In the traditional American manner of the beat poets like [Allen] Ginsberg, this author and poet got on stage for recitations and lectures given in a loud voice. And one day – it was still at the beginning of the seventies – she began to be accompanied by a guitarist: Lenny Kaye, a rock critic friend who already had a background as a musician, having played the bass for various groups such as the Vandals and Man Ray. The passage was smoothed between the electric poetry and the rock and roll. Patti had a flaming passion, a violent energy, a dose of exhibitionism indispensable to every career of a star ... and ... that not at all negligible quality, the profoundly American need to succeed, the desire to make it at any cost....

She also possessed the physical strength to succeed. Patiently made over the years, Patti applied herself to create in her body and her face the same energy and poetry as existed inside her. Everyone is born with the face and the body provided by nature. From there on, it's up to each person to play with it, to fashion it. Patti had behind her a history as a scrawny little girl, neither pretty nor ugly, a frustrated fan of Dylan and the Stones ... who then, suddenly, one day moved with self-assurance on to the rock stage because she had finally become what she had dreamed! The pale intensity of her look and the sexual magnetism were both united in an extraordinary innocence. Her walk had the imprint of undeniable elegance and she modelled her look after Keith Richards: the hollow cheeks, the dark and tangled tresses, a certain rapid contraction of the facial muscles ... and it was as if that sudden appearance of Patti Smith had been prepared by years of patient work on herself.

Marjorie Alessandrini
Le Rock au Feminin, 1980

Madonna

The last time we saw you in photographs, you were like Marilyn Monroe. It was like the image of a superstar, of a myth, and now all at once you've stopped all that.

Because I am like that. Because I like to go from one thing to the other. I like to show one facet, then another radically different one and make people understand that they're always dealing with the same person. For me, it is essential.... The problem of being a star is that you are placed straight away on a pedestal and that, from that time on, you no longer have the right to be a human being, to cry, to laugh at stupid things. That's the reason that I knock the image, so that people will reflect. I'm just a girl, that's all. I believe that people are surprised to see that I am intelligent and funny.

Marie Colmant
Libération, 14 May 1991

Children are very aware of sex. It's not a secret. I think what's wrong is people say they don't want children to know about sex or teach them about sex, safe sex, sex education. That's a mistake. That's why AIDS is spreading in the heterosexual community very swiftly right now, because straight people think they can't get it. That's bullshit. I think that's why there's so many teenagers that are pregnant, because no one wants to talk about sex. But meanwhile, the kids are all going out and having it. I

think it shouldn't be something that we sweep under the rug. I think that we should all just admit that our children are having sex at very young ages, so let's talk about it. Let's talk about safe sex, let's discuss it. Let's sit down with the kids and say, 'Do you want to have a child right now, are you ready to have that responsibility? Would you like to have venereal disease or AIDS, or whatever? You have to talk to your children about these things, because they exist, so what's the point of pretending that they don't? It's worse if you pretend that it doesn't exist.

Interview by Simon Bates
Classic Interviews: 25 Rock Greats in their own Words, 1992,
edited by Jeff Simpson

Annie Lennox

'It's a game, and one I don't really want to play,' she says of the celebrity whirl. 'But these are very self-promotional times, and I accept that this is what I'm doing now, promoting Eurythmics, promoting myself. It's what I have to enter into if I want us to be out there in the market-place, but it's a circus too ... finding your work reduced to "Annie took to the stage in a mini-skirt", it's bullshit.'

With Madonna, she shares the distinction of being one of pop's most skilful manipulators of image this decade. But while Madonna, though presenting herself as an independent free-thinker, has reinforced an aura of sexual desirability, Lennox has taken more chances. Brave enough to appear deliberately unattractive by conventional standards, she has interpreted her music in guises ranging from neurotic housewife to predatory transvestite. The daring she has shown, particularly on video ... has helped her bring a rare element of subversion to the often desperately narcissistic medium of pop.

'We're all afraid of not being beautiful or fashionable enough,' she judges.'I know I can look beautiful on film or in a photograph, but that I can also look really dreadful. So I can play with those two extremes. This is a very male-dominated industry and a woman's potential can easily be blocked. Not too many have been allowed to emerge as anything other than some sort of sex object, but I always knew I would never be satisfied by being presented as an attractive girl singer.'

Interview by Alan Jackson
Observer, 17 September 1989

A female record executive speaks out

Perhaps the real answer is that boys just don't want girls spoiling their party, as this story from Ann Kelly [Virgin's former sales manager] suggests:

'Sales managers and directors from all the companies used to get together every six months to talk about the industry. Christmas was coming up, probably in my second year as sales manager, and at the previous meeting they had discussed it and set a date. But the organizer had changed the date and the venue, and didn't tell me – a certain group of them had chatted and decided "Ann'll not want to come". They basically wanted a good night out with the boys. It wouldn't have bothered me, quite honestly, if they'd have come out and said that. But I was talking to someone at CBS and he mentioned it accidentally – I was, of course, very annoyed and phoned up the guy. In fact, Brian Mulligan, who

then ran *Record Business,* put a bit in his column saying, "Is Ann Kelly giving the industry chauvinist ties for Christmas?" Of course, I didn't! But the following year, they made sure I'd been invited.'

Sue Steward and Sheryl Garratt
Signed, Sealed and Delivered: True Life Stories of Women in Pop, 1984

Tina Turner and *Private Dancer*

It was 1983 when you started to make this album. Where was your career going then?
It had started to do quite well. My manager, Roger Davies, had organized a European tour and he wanted me to go out with a record, even if it wasn't a hit, to release something and say I was promoting it....

I didn't have material, I barely had a record company, I didn't have a producer, didn't have anything, I was just starting out on my own.

You had no real direction in mind?
I had no direction. We were just trying to get songs for an album, because we needed an album then. We were following a hit single ['Let's Stay Together'] and we weren't prepared, so it was like whatever we could get....

You know this album was done in two weeks?...

This album marked a time in my life. My first Number 1 song ['What's Love Got To Do With It'] came out of this album. This was a hit album for me, back on my own after close to seven years just working clubs and things.... Each time I look at it [her painting of the album cover], I look at my success.

John Pidgeon
Classic Albums: Interviews from the Radio One Series, 1991

The twilight of the stars

Even stars die. Or else they fade away, suffering from alienation. Brian Wilson, founder of the Beach Boys, underwent psychiatric treatment. Bob Dylan wore himself out with endless tours. Led Zeppelin closed up shop. But only their greatest moments will live on in our memory.

The Beach Boys. Brian Wilson stands at the back.

Brian Wilson

I was with Brian Wilson the first time he surfed. It was Father's Day, 20 June 1976.... There was something mystical and childlike about him; he radiated an aura, a magnetic presence that drew people to him. He turned and looked out to the ocean, and the distance in his eyes made the expanse of the Pacific seem small.

But those eyes. Those cold blue eyes were terrified. Brian Wilson was somewhere else, struggling hard to be in touch with what was happening on the beach, but from the other side of a psychic glass wall. Brian Wilson is schizophrenic. As the producer-composer of the Beach Boys, Brian, along with his brothers Dennis and Carl Wilson, cousin Mike Love and friend Al Jardine, had proselytized the legendary California good life around the world for fifteen years, but for twelve of those years Brian had been on a reclusive psychological odyssey....

At the unheard-of cost of $70,000 for production, *Pet Sounds* was brilliant – not only for its innovation, but for its melancholy innocence. A searching album about growing up and the pain involved in the realities of adulthood, *Pet Sounds* is introverted, thoughtful and childishly curious. There is something odd about the album, lonely and alienated. The tone of the album went beyond sensitive into a realm of something nearly pathetic – the whimper of a tortured young mind.

Steven Gaines
The True Story of the Beach Boys, 1988

Bob Dylan

Why is it that no rock star who has continued rocking into middle age has done so without becoming sentimental, repetitious, embarrassing or, in Dylan's case, impertinent? From the moment that the living legend took to the stage it was evident that here was business he wanted accomplished with the minimum of effort. Sounding like one

of those talent competition impersonators who have to tell you who they are 'doing' – 'that was Mister Tommy Cooper, bless him, and now do you remember Mister Bobby Dylan?' – it appeared to be as much as Dylan could bear to grumble out his lyrics at all. By the time he reached 'The lonesome death of Hattie Carroll', he was gasping each word as though playing a dying man trying to communicate the name of his murderer in an amateur production of a thriller.

John Peel
'More Music: Dylan at Wembley'
Observer, 18 October 1987

Led Zeppelin

Jimmy Page's group was made up of John Paul Jones, John Bonham and, of course, Robert Plant, whose shrill, dominating voice would put a stamp on a dozen albums. The Page/Plant couple quickly became a volcanic pair of young divorcés from Liverpool. Sprouting out of the blues roots which it never denied, Led Zeppelin became the champion of progressive, elaborate, belaboured heavy rock (Deep Purple? Ha!), not hesitating, if needed, to play the role of sonic Marco Polos *(Physical Graffiti)*. Around 1975, the group was the sovereign of a realm built of huge bricks condemned to collapse under the weight of their omnipotence.

The end would be more abrupt. As with Keith Moon of the Who and Bon Scott of AC/DC, Led Zeppelin, one day in 1980, surrendered up its sacrifice to the rock legend: John Bonham was prematurely placed in his coffin. Deprived of the hammer of their stock, the surviving trio abandoned their position on high to several pathetic pillagers (like the band Kingdom Come) and stepped back from the fray in a manner befitting their rank. Page went astray. Jones tinkered about *(The Mission)*, Bonham had played on Friday the 13th *(Jason 2: The Return)* and the great Robert rescaled the ramparts in June 1982 *(Pictures at Eleven)*. He would repeat the effort, with a somewhat faltering and devitalized heavy metal sound, on the next album and on average every two years, standing up to the attacks and challenges which the young mocking metal lackeys launched at him.

Gilles Renault
Libération, 22 May 1992

Heavy metal

Hard rock has had a hard life. Born twenty-five years ago with the talented guitarists of the Yardbirds and their Holy Trinity of Clapton, Beck and Page, it has become harder over the years to see in it any of its blues roots.

The saga of Deep Purple

At the end of the sixties the British invented heavy metal, with its bluesy strains.

They were a supergroup whose imprint would remain indelible throughout the seventies – a key group, in fact, whose avatars and metamorphoses (Ian Gillian Group, Whitesnake, Rainbow) have brought renown or still bring fame to the world arena of heavy metal music. The story of Deep Purple begins roughly at the same time as that of Led Zeppelin, in 1968. However at that time, Jimmy Page's dirigible was well ahead. While Led Zeppelin gave hard rock its first masterpiece, Deep Purple – organized around the pianist Jon Lord and the guitarist Ritchie Blackmore – confined itself to an exclusive repertoire of pompously arranged reprises in the wake of Vanilla Fudge and the baroque rock of Nice. This vaguely bastardized form of rock taken from classicism was in fashion at the end of the sixties. The first albums of Deep Purple quickly established the group on the British and, above all, the American charts (more than a quarter of a million albums sold in four months in the United States!). On stage, these somewhat stilted musical forms had a tendency to blur a toccata in favour of a sumptuous sonic massacre. Ritchie Blackmore, a disciple of Jeff Beck, slayed his amplifiers with great guitar riffs, while Jon Lord played his organ in the tradition of Keith Emerson in an orgy of decibels.

Philippe Blanchet
Heavy Metal, 1985

Dee Snider (Twisted Sister).

Led Zeppelin

In a field of monsters Led Zeppelin were the true leviathans of rock. While their accumulated album sales may not match those of today's biggest selling acts they were, in their time, quite simply the biggest act on the planet.

Ritchie Blackmore (Deep Purple).

Led Zeppelin.

Other acts sold records – Led Zeppelin set standards.... The first band recording was titled simply *Led Zeppelin* and released in early 1969 ... having been recorded in a mere thirty hours. It was a blockbusting explosion of heavy blues that currently serves to re-emphasize the roots of heavy metal. It won rave reviews in Britain ... and the album rapidly went gold. In December it was followed by *Led Zeppelin II*, truly a landmark album with the classic 'Whole Lotta Love' remaining a standard to this day. Within less than two years Led Zeppelin rocketed to the very top of the tree, with enormous success on both sides of the Atlantic.

Zeppelin spent much of 1970 on the road. In May they recorded *Led Zeppelin III* which further refined their approach to heavy rock yet exposed the more folk-orientated influences of Page and Plant. Released in October, the

album was a colossal success, but still nobody was prepared for the epochal *Led Zeppelin IV* which appeared just over a year later. This set new standards in the field of heavy rock from the thunder of 'Black Dog' to the epic 'Stairway to Heaven'....

Paul Suter
HM A–Z: The Ultimate Heavy Metal Encyclopedia, 1985

The eighties

Current heavy metal has a thriving subgenre – even more extreme than most heavy metal – that is obsessed by death and destruction. The heirs of Judas Priest, [Ozzy] Osbourne's Black Sabbath and other apocalypse-mongering heavy metal bands, cross-bred with the momentum and anti-pop ferocity of punk-rock, are the speed-metal or thrash bands of the 1980s. They bring portents of doom – personal and global – in words barked between jackhammer jolts of guitar, and they've become too popular to shrug off. Metallica ... has sold a million copies of its latest album *...And Justice for All*, in less than a month; Anthrax's new *State of Euphoria* and Slayer's *South of Heaven* are also selling well.

Speed-metal has established its own musical and verbal conventions. More often than not, it pounds along at breakneck tempos, stopping and starting at irregular intervals like a fibrillating heart. It's anything but droning and hypnotic; its rhythms are choppy and memory-defying, calling for high-powered virtuosity and delivering new impact with every lurch. Yet for all the tricky stops and starts, the harmonies are utterly simple. Most songs sputter along in every guitarist's first chord, E minor, and melodies are chanted or barked in a narrow range. So the music is both explosive and constricted – just the way a teenager can feel much of the time.

It's what speed-metal bands are saying, though, that gains them attention and notoriety....

A typical album includes songs about nuclear holocaust, dying in combat, captivity, turning into an automaton, going mad, about losing control and going on a rampage – tales of destruction, compulsion, power turned to evil ends, often envisioned in gory detail. There are also likely to be songs about outcasts and victims, the casualties of authority and power, along with denunciations of hypocrisy and assertions of independence. And some songs address suicidal feelings....

Some things are missing, too. Among them are love, romance, and sexuality; speed-metal bands don't sexualize violence the way slasher films or 'Miami Vice' do. While there are accusations and pronouncements, there's very little moralizing....

[The] speed-metal bands add the defiance and anti-authoritarian sentiments that have always been a part of rock and roll. Their messages aren't demagogic commands to follow the leader or to go on destructive binges. They urge listeners to think for themselves, to insist on independence and the truth, to question authority and battle coercion.... [Rock] that tells teenagers that they face a dangerous, irrational, brutal world tells them the unsanitized truth. It also tells each worried teenager that others have been terrified and enraged.... [Speed-metal] bands strike a chord with millions of teenagers because they reflect what's on their minds – and the songs tell them they are not alone.

Jon Pareles
'Speed-Metal: Extreme, Yes; Evil, No'
The New York Times
25 September 1988

Metallica

Fans of intelligent music have to get used to it: hard rock crops up there more and more. But be careful. When one says 'hard' one is not just talking about the Scorpions, Dio or other aging and largely FMized drudges, but the new wave of metal. This crowd of groups, from Soundgarden to Mary My Path passing through Faith No More, Prong and White Zombies, have abandoned most of the grotesque cliches of the genre – skin-tight imitation leopard leatherette pants, an assortment of faces of half-witted perverts, grandiloquent and obese albums – all benefiting a global approach favouring energy and brutal 'efficiency', the hot air of the instrumental hemming and hawing, and nonsensical medieval dragon imagery. By way of distinctive omen, little remains today of these formula hard rockers but their basically cretinous lyrics and their long hair.

All this in order to get to what? To Metallica, the missing link between hard and punk and the incontestable precursor of the metallic new age. Since 1983 this quartet of Americans based in San Francisco violently stated the foundations of speed metal with *Kill 'Em All,* their first album of noise with flourishes. At the beginning, their T-shirt–black jeans–sneakers style was identical to that of the international 'kid' style and they were equally seduced by the slogans of 'Kill Bon Jovi' and 'More Beer'. But their guitar work soon established the group as saviours of a dying metal style.

Metallica's recognition grew when they participated in the Monsters of Rock US tour two years ago where, performing between the Scorpions and Van Halen, they had no trouble calling attention to themselves as rising stars....

A Metallica concert is more than two hours of noisy energy as steadfast as it is invigorating. It is based on the (sexual) alternations between tension and hesitation and is played by the four heavy outlaws, who perform on an undecorated set consisting of stage curtains hanging in ruins over the amplifiers.

With only few rare 'solos' there is a minimum of verbal exchange with the public, as if to ascertain that they're just among ourselves. On the whole, they pick up from the Ramones and from Motörhead, but with a completely different set of references. As their 1987 mini-LP *Garage Days Re-Revisited* attests, the band remade in their unique style some songs by disappointing 1970s hard rock groups from Diamondhead to Budgie. We will have to seriously rethink this music – this usually cretinous music for

J ames Hetfield (Metallica).

morons served up by mental halfwits. Metallica is something different.... And their guitarist Kirk Hammett, seen back-stage after the concert, is absolutely delicious!

Laurence Romance
Libération, 21 May 1990

The eighties

The decade was marked by materialism. Some succumbed to the rewards of success; others turned to political involvement. After a chilly period marked by the 'cold wave' and the domination of synthesizer groups, rock little by little rediscovered the simplicity of electric guitars.

Pygmalion and his masterpiece

Quincy Jones produced the album Thriller *by Michael Jackson.*

Q: Do you think that the success of Michael Jackson will help other black

INCLUDES THE SMASH HITS
I JUST CAN'T STOP LOVING YOU
BAD

artists in the United States?

QUINCY JONES: Each time that a black artist is recognized for his talent and his success, and that carves out a place for him within an industry – show business for example – it is a fundamental success for all blacks. Take the example of Michael Jackson, Richard Pryor or Eddie Murphy – their individual successes opened the path for other artists. That will create a new race of black directors, of black scriptwriters, of black actors. The fact that today Richard Pryor can with his name alone get a budget of $40 million for a film, for blacks it is the proof that everything is possible, and that gives them confidence and energy....

The success of Michael Jackson largely exceeds the framework of show business. He has galvanized all the black population. It is a political and social success. Don't forget that if blacks don't succeed more often, it is not because of a lack of talent – it is only because of the colour of their skins. For the thirty years that I have been in the record industry, it has always been said that black performers could aspire to success on only a limited scale. Michael Jackson finally broke the stereotypes. His sales figures have broken through the existing standards set in the record industry, and at the same time that success has helped to break through the racism of certain black radio stations and of MTV. Each black person knows that he must be the best, and for that to happen, it is necessary that he extend himself. In succeeding, he will help all blacks to succeed.

Michèle Halberstadt
Libération, 11 March 1984

Big business

Quite apart from its considerable musical merits, *Thriller* defined both a strategy and a standard for success in the 1980s.... You might be a brilliant songwriter and a stunning musician, but after *Thriller*'s ground-breaking videos ... you'd better be something of an actor, too – or at least a pretty face.... After *Thriller*, platinum sales – earned by selling a million or more copies – were a prerequisite for stardom....

To a greater degree than ever before marketing – the creation and selling of an image – became an essential component of an artist's success. Videos, video compilations, long-form videos, corporate sponsorships, product endorsements, T-shirts, book deals, interviews, television appearances, movie tie-ins, songs for soundtracks – all that began to envelop what was once considered a rebel's world, the world you chose because you had no other choice or you hated the idea of working for the man, because you wanted independence and freedom and nothing less, because you wanted that greatest of all possible goods, that most sublime of all possible states: to be a rock & roll star.

By the mid-1980s, rock & roll was well on its way to becoming terminally safe. Joining a rock band had become a career move like any other, about as rebellious as taking a business degree, and, if you got lucky, more lucrative....

Artists seemed to be tripping over themselves ... to sell out, to lease their songs to sell products, to put their dreams in the service of commerce.

Anthony DeCurtis
'The Eighties'
Present Tense: Rock & Roll Culture
Edited by Anthony DeCurtis, 1992

U2 on success

Success to us was like the big bad wolf, I couldn't believe that I was actually getting paid for doing this thing that I'd do. I *had* to do it, and I'd do it for free, and we just didn't know what to do with it. And then in the end, we were getting a *lot* for it. So from where I was coming from, and the way I was brought up, I wasn't quite prepared for it, and all the shit that comes with it. I would have been a socialist in the way that I was brought up, my father voted Labour, and ... we turned success into the big bad wolf.

I think one of the reasons that we were so uptight in the '80s – we were kind of staring down the '80s and the whole Material Girl thing, greed-is-good and everything – and we were being photographed in this Amish-Shaker-Quaker kind of way, and just going the opposite way. And yet we were getting shit-loads of dough for this, and it was kinda f—ing us up a bit.

And I think that now we've realized that rock 'n' roll is, in a way, ridiculous – and that's part of why we're into it.

Bono of U2
Interview by Stuart Bailie
New Musical Express, 13 June 1992

Morrissey, the ex-Smiths leader, on being famous

Is crime another interest of yours?

'Well I think it always has been, not actively, but a fascinating subject. I've never stolen. I'm interested in the sense of celebrity, even on the level of murder, and the fame attached to grizzly crimes. I often wonder why people who commit such crimes are treated like celebrities, it doesn't do the crime rate much good does it?...

'I think it's wrong that people who do notorious things receive a heightened sense of attention, but there will always be people like Michael Ryan and the whole boring Rambo thing.

'The fame attached is part of the chase for people because there is such a pressure on most people to produce proof that they have lived, if you like, leave something behind. And it's not enough merely to reproduce. I think people are obsessed with fame these days. Everybody wants to leave their mark, nobody wants to be an ordinary plodding citizen. And the lengths that some people will go to are quite enormous, for better, for worse.'

Interview by James Brown
New Musical Express, 11 February 1989

Today Morrissey is in a unique, if equivocal, position. He is a performer whose celebrity outweighs his record sales. This has made him nervous; like many people who have turned themselves into the 'living sign' of celebrity, he flirts with the media, while being obsessively private. He lives alone in a suburb of south Manchester and has 'a secret sect of friends. I find it very hard unravelling and getting to know new people'.

'Fame, fatal fame,' he sang in 1986; 'It can play hideous tricks on the brain.'

more community-based values. Thus, the 'rave culture' was born in Britain and spread through the rest of the world.

It allowed each person – regardless of age, of social background or of the colour of their skin – to escape, for the space of one night to where time stands still, to where the harrowing rules of reality which manage modern western lives don't exist, and to where one could capture again the instinct of pleasure: to be together, tribally united by dance in the same vessel, rocked by the fantastic energy of the house. It is a music which, in functioning without or almost without 'figureheads', has completely perverted the concept even of 'stars' since they are no longer on the stage – empowered by the DJs – but on the floor....

The whole house music sound arouses in its detractors the same incomprehension, the same reactions of slightly frightened rejection that punk rock and acid rock met in their time. The fear is that raves would essentially assemble an audience of druggies who would come together to dance till they dropped to a music that 'just sounded all the same'.

The criticism is obviously unjustified: from the garage sound to the ambient sound, from deep house to techno, house music is so varied in its conception that it offers exhilarating possibilities to those desirous of mastering the machinery of their creative imagination....

Laurence Romance
Les Inrockuptibles
March 1992

Rock rediscovered

As in Memphis and Liverpool not so long ago, rock blossomed outside the big cities in the eighties. In the United States, it was created around universities with their resources of radios, clubs and record stores – the famous 'college circuit'.

The B-52s and REM were born on the campus of the University of Georgia in Athens. In Britain, Manchester was the centre – it had always engendered excellent musicians (Graham Nash, Joe Cocker, the Buzzcocks, Lloyd Cole), and in a short period of time it became the mecca of new rock.

In the wake of Joy Division and its successor New Order, a strong neo-psychedelic current developed at the end of the eighties with the Happy Mondays, James, Stone Roses and the Charlatans, who took their name from the popular group in San Francisco in the sixties and used the same kind of light-show-based stage show.

More and more, rock turned inwards and studied its past, adoring that which had burned brightly just a short time before. Through contact with other music, it crossbred, integrating all the invigorating contemporary black elements like rap and 'house music' from Chicago. The exchanges went both ways: Prince and Michael Jackson had conquered the white audience with melodies and stage shows. They designed an image to seduce the audience, but without denying their closest influences like Jimi Hendrix and the Motown sound.

Today rock searches through its own history, mixing and remixing all that it has invented in forty years while waiting for the next revolution.

Alain Dister
September 1992

Experimentation and innovation

In the world of rock some giants stand out in terms of their creative ability and technical expertise. In many different ways these musicians have brought something new to rock and roll.

J imi Hendrix's *Are You Experienced* record cover.

Jimi Hendrix and Eric Clapton: guitar heroes

Throughout the late sixties, Hendrix rivalled Eric Clapton as rock's number one guitar hero, and it was an index of how times had changed that the American had to go to Britain to establish his reputation....

In Britain ... Hendrix recorded as his first single the song 'Hey Joe' which he had heard by the Leaves in Los Angeles earlier in the year. Mysterious, menacing and dynamically very well paced, the record in effect picked up on the blues where the Rolling Stones had left the idiom after topping the British charts with 'Little Red Rooster' in 1964, and 'Hey Joe' by the Jimi Hendrix Experience made the British top ten early in 1967. Just as Britain was beginning to feel the reverberations of the drug culture of San Francisco, here was a young black man from the West Coast with frizzy hair, outrageously colourful clothes and no inhibitions about using the guitar as a sexual symbol.

Vocally, Hendrix was no great shakes, but when he found a song that suited his more-or-less conversational delivery, he filled in all the meaning and emotions with flickering guitar work. Where Clapton played with attack and tension, Hendrix tended to take his time and stay relaxed; who was 'better' was a matter of personal taste, but the rivalry helped to focus attention on blues guitar-playing in general, and even led to some attention for the originators.

Charlie Gillett
*The Sound of the City:
The Rise of Rock and Roll,* 1983

Pink Floyd and *The Dark Side of the Moon* (1973)

As you said earlier, electronic instruments were in their infancy, but you were obviously excited by their possibilities.
Oh, absolutely, yes. We were all of us very keen on the electronic stuff. They were very very basic, these early synthesizers, and in fact for a long time we had them without actually knowing how to make the keyboards work and play notes. We spent an awful long time – and actually became rather good at – using them as sound effects' machines; creating noises, explosions, wind and strange things. But it took a lot longer before we actually learned how to play them. They weren't like modern synthesizers where you plug them in, turn them on and play, a keyboard and notes come out. You actuallly had to program them up to play notes. You had to set the octaves in by turning a litttle knob round and patching it up properly and connecting up the keyboard. I think we'd had them for over a year before we even knew that you could play notes, rather than noises and straight drones and things....

Do you have any theories as to why this record became such a monster? It's more than just a big record.
It must have captured a spirit of that moment or something. There's something in there for everyone. There's a song that means something to most people in that album. But to be absolutely honest, I don't really understand why it did quite as well as it did do.

John Pidgeon
Classic Albums: Interviews from the Radio One Series, 1991

David Bowie: *Aladdin Sane*

Bowie's approach is always intellectual. This latest album, *Aladdin Sane*, proves it more perhaps than any other. Bowie's music should always be listened to ironically. Here it is a confrontation of contemporary attitudes with neo-fifties accents, cabaret revival, but also a Cecil Taylor–like piano. But Bowie's 'musical intelligence' reaches such a degree of perfection that the music of *Aladdin Sane* never seems like a series of collages or an amalgam. On the contrary, it constitutes an important contribution to the new rock and roll aesthetic.

There is nothing whorish or vulgarly easy in this sequence of the works. Instead, the musical whole presents an ambitious sonic approach. If 'Watch That Man' is in the tradition of *Ziggy Stardust*, with 'Aladdin Sane' and 'Time', Bowie takes a new step in his sonic research. Thus Mike Gargon's piano echoes Mick Ronson's guitar in the Yardbirds. For 'Lady Grinning Soul', the sentimental accents disappear into a clear modern approach in their utilization of sounds. Moreover, Bowie remains an extraordinary chronicler of rock, showcasing in his lyrics all of the legend, all of the history of this music. 'Panic in Detroit' is an homage to the great era of John Sinclair's White Panther Party. There are also the precise references to the world of 'decadent' stars in 'Cracked Actors', which is very similar to Lou Reed's lyrics, for example. 'The Prettiest Star' is an old song written at the same time as *Space Oddity* and serves as the transition between 'Time' and a very personalized version of the Stones' 'Let's Spend the Night Together'. There again, the romantic quality disappears in a wild but controlled din.

The pleasure of this album is subtle: there are no disruptions. Bowie succeeds, in essence, to place side by side in *Aladdin Sane* songs like 'Time' and the already famous 'Jean Genie' in a manner which seems at ease. *Aladdin Sane* has the ambition to prove that Bowie is more than a phenomenon of fashion but a true 'synthesizer-creator' of the seventies. Who could pretend that he has not succeeded, except those for whom the blues did not exist before the Stones, those for whom there had never been an Elvis Presley before the Beatles? Bowie is a genius, like all the greats of rock.

Paul Alessandrini
Rock & Folk, 1973

Sex Pistols: *Never Mind the Bollocks Here's the Sex Pistols*

Finally. It's been such a long time.... Such a long time for what? It's difficult to explain: I've heard a lot of good records in the last ten years and a reasonable number [of good ones] are released each year, but this time it's ... truly different. We don't give a damn whether the Pistols are punk or something else. Forget about that. The only thing that counts is that they are the Pistols. Not only do they stand head and shoulders above the best groups of the new wave (which is beginning to be the holy dumping ground for fashionable ghosts), but above all they are unique. Johnny Rotten is the most charismatic personality to appear on the rock scene for a long time.

He is also an extraordinary (in the most exact definition of the term) singer. His unique phrasing, this manner of drawing out words, of cutting them off with what you think is a smile – this voice which one could call a bleat, if it were not so triumphant, would make him an absolute innovator.

But he is much more than that. He is terribly real. He is not duped by the punk nonsense or by the star trip which is awaiting him, and he lives each word of his songs. The words of the Pistols are important, but in the manner of real rock lyrics: they only make complete sense in their context. This aggression, this rage, have we accumulated so much frustration?

The shiver that possesses the listener to these Pistols has one meaning; rock and roll finds in it suddenly something new – neither explicit or explainable, of course. It carries the impalpable sense of the era, 1977, the time of [the German terrorist group] Baader-Meinhof, and it is not a coincidence. The strange romanticism of a desperate hope.... Eleven songs (they appear in a different order in the English version and are completed by a twelfth, 'Sub-mission'). It is difficult and useless to make a choice. None of them let up on the implacable intensity of the ensemble.

This record allows no chance. Listening to two sharp sides is incredibly exhausting, it empties all energy, confronts a too visceral and total truth to be explained here. Don't make Rotten a hero or a star – this record must be a personal experience, it can only be that. And you can't ignore it. In any case, I hope that for you.

Hervé Muller
Rock & Folk, 1977

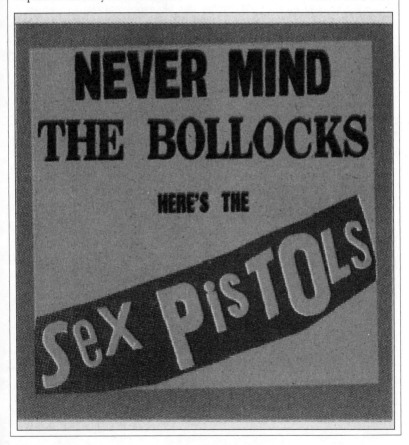

The surveillance of a soul rebel

Years after Bob Marley's death, journalist Timothy White reveals how this hero to so many may have seemed a dangerous man to a powerful few.

From steelpan to spooge, from mento to soca, the Caribbean Basin has always been a region steeped in topical music that could pierce the conscience just as surely as it could spark the spirit. And in Bob Marley's homeland, his music drew from the living heritage of those who had played and sung before him, to the point where his reggae became far greater than the sum of its influences. It grew from a cultural fad into a fierce act of faith and will, and then blossomed into a force of nature.

The Third World is most of the world, and by the time of his death in 1981 it was difficult to locate a corner of it where people had no knowledge of Bob and his message. But in Africa, it was impossible. From Nigeria, to Angola, to Zimbabwe, to Mozambique, to South Africa, his image and his music were carried through the streets by citizens struggling for freedom and self-determination, because he sang about and fervently supported the essential justice of all such movements. It's become fashionable since his passing to put a rigid political interpretation on Marley's outpourings, to label him a liberal of a particular cast, or a socialist, or even a closet Marxist. The facts do not support this conjecture. He had no dogmatic political beliefs....

At the time of the assassination attempt in Kingston on Friday, December 3, 1976, Marley was well on the way to becoming one of the best-known black figures of modern times....

Bob Marley was powerful politically, largely because he never codified or exercised any of his implicit power. Music was his life, and he had no hidden agendas. These are among the many reasons he may have been watched closely by eyes besides those of his admirers. And why those other eyes perhaps judged him a dangerous man.

There is no shortage of unanswered questions about the attempt on Marley's life. It's become well-known that Bob had enemies in the ghettos of West Kingston; Jamaican Labor Party (JLP) badmen in Tivoli Gardens and other strongholds of Opposition leader Edward Seaga were openly disgruntled that Bob seemed to be siding with Prime Minister Michael Manley's People's National Party (PNP) by consenting to appear at the upcoming PNP-sponsored "Smile Jamaica" festival. It's also known that Marley had inadvertently become involved in a fixed-race scandal at Caymanas Park Race Track.... When some of Marley's associates left the island with the loot ... Bob was the highly visible figure to whom the duped went for retribution. But there is the lingering theory that most of the internal and external political forces vying for control of Jamaica's destiny at this juncture were willing to let the chips fall where they may – providing they fell immediately and DECISIVELY. If a volatile, unbought figure like Marley should run afoul of his shantytown chums and become a martyr, the reasoning went, then so be it. If he never played another concert in Jamaica, that was okay too. But the bottom line was that he would be best out of the way. On one side of the mounting firestorm in West Kingston were jealous/overzealous PNP goons who had compelled Marley to appear at the Smile Jamaica concert; on the other side was gathered a distempered JLP-affiliated group of gravely disgruntled race-fixers from Tivoli Gardens.

The [JLP] gunmen came for Bob Marley in two white Datsuns on a Friday evening at approximately 8:45.... Though wounded in the nighttime raid ... Marley went on to perform at the Sunday show. [Island Records head Chris] Blackwell made arrangements for a private jet to pick up Bob and friend Neville Garrick in a remote corner of Norman Manley Airport at 5:30 Monday morning. Bob was to remain guarded by plainclothes government security officials until he was safely aboard the plane....

However, when Bob and Neville awoke in the pre-dawn hours on Monday and began preparing to leave for the airport, there were NO security police to be seen.... Eventually, Neville and Bob had no recourse but to drive down the mountain, devoid of any police protection. They entered the closed Norman Manley Airport ... and found their own way to the waiting jet. On the outskirts of the air field, a few soldiers in jeeps watched through binoculars but, curiously, kept their distance. Shaken and confused by the surreal setting, Bob and Neville gingerly crossed the tarmac, climbed aboard the aircraft, closed the door behind themselves and took off with the flight crew.

At roughly that same point, unbeknownst to Marley and Garrick, a confidential CIA/State Department telegram was moving on the government wires to the State Department in Washington, as well as to the American embassies in Kingston, Nassau and other Caribbean locations, offering a four-part synopsis of the ghoulish weekend developments in Jamaica. The communiqué's tagline: SUBJECT: REGGAE STAR SHOT; MOTIVE PROBABLY POLITICAL.

Timothy White, 1989

DISCOGRAPHY

Record labels, in a constant state of flux, have not been added; an album is best identified by its artist and title.

CHAPTER 1

Charles, Ray, *World of Ray Charles*
Cochran, Eddie, *The Eddie Cochran Singles Album*
Crudup, Arthur, *The Father of Rock and Roll*
Domino, Fats, *Golden Greats*
Haley, Bill, *Golden Hits*
Holly, Buddy, *Complete Buddy Holly*
Howlin' Wolf, *The Howlin' Wolf Album*
Johnson, Robert, *King of the Delta Blues Singers*
King, B. B., *Greatest Hits*
Lewis, Jerry Lee, *The Greatest Live Show on Earth*
———, *Original Golden Hits*
———, *Live at the Star Club Hamburg*
Orbison, Roy, *Monumental Hits*
Perkins, Carl, *Original Greatest Hits*
Presley, Elvis, *The Sun Sessions*
———, *Legendary Performer*
Vincent, Gene, *Gene Vincent and His Blue Caps*
Waters, Muddy, *The Best of Muddy Waters*
Williams, Hank, *40 Greatest Hits*

CHAPTER 2

Back to Mono (anthology produced by Phil Spector)
Berry, Chuck, *Chuck Berry*
Best of Doo-Wop Ballads
Best of Doo-Wop Uptempo
Cooke, Sam, *Live at the Harlem Square Club*
Darin, Bobby, *Ultimate Bobby Darin*
The Drifters, *Golden Hits*
Everly Brothers, *The Everly Brothers*
Little Richard, *All-Time Hits*
Nelson, Ricky, *Legendary Masters*
The Platters, *Two Decades of Hits*
Wilson, Jackie, *My Golden Favourites*

CHAPTER 3

The Animals, *Best of the Animals*
The Beatles, *Please Please Me*
———, *With the Beatles*
———, *Revolver*
———, *Rubber Soul*
Beck, Jeff, *Beck-Ola*
———, *Truth*
Brown, James, *The Best of James Brown*
Franklin, Aretha, *Lady Soul*
Gaye, Marvin, *What's Going On*
The Hollies, *The Best of the Hollies*

The Kinks, *The Kinks*
Mann, Manfred, *The Best of Manfred Mann*
Morrison, Van, *Astral Weeks*
Redding, Otis, *Otis Blue*
The Rolling Stones, *The Rolling Stones*
———, *The Rolling Stones No. 2*
———, *Beggar's Banquet*
———, *Aftermath*
The Who, *The Who Sell Out*
———, *My Generation*
Wonder, Stevie, *Greatest Hits*
The Yardbirds, *Five Live Yardbirds*

CHAPTER 4

Baez, Joan, *Farewell, Angelina*
The Band, *Music From Big Pink*
The Beach Boys, *Pet Sounds*
———, *Surfin' USA*
Big Brother and the Holding Company, *Cheap Thrills*
Brown, James, *Live at the Apollo*
Buffalo Springfield, *Buffalo Springfield Again*
The Byrds, *The Byrds' Greatest Hits*
———, *Mr Tambourine Man*
The Doors, *LA Woman*
———, *Strange Days*
Dylan, Bob, *Blonde on Blonde*
———, *Bringing It All Back Home*
———, *Highway 61 Revisited*
The Four Tops, *Super Hits*
Franklin, Aretha, *Aretha's Greatest Hits*
———, *Ten Years of Gold*
Gaye, Marvin, *What's Going On*
The Grateful Dead, *Live Dead*
———, *Workingman's Dead*
The Jefferson Airplane, *Surrealistic Pillow*
Ochs, Phil, *I Ain't Marchin' Anymore*
Robinson, Smokey, and the Miracles, *Pure Smokey*
Ross, Diana, and the Supremes, *Anthology*
Sam and Dave, *Best of Sam and Dave*
Simon and Garfunkel, *Bridge Over Troubled Water*
The Temptations, *Greatest Hits*
The Velvet Underground, *The Velvet Underground and Nico*
———, *White Light/White Heat*
Wonder, Stevie, *Stevie Wonder's Greatest Hits*
Zappa, Frank, *Hot Rats*
———, *Uncle Meat*

CHAPTER 5

The Allman Brothers Band, *Live At Fillmore East*
The Beatles, *Sgt Pepper's Lonely Hearts Club Band*
Bowie, David, *Aladdin Sane*

————, *The Rise and Fall of Ziggy Stardust and the Spiders from Mars*
Canned Heat, *The Very Best of Canned Heat*
Cohen, Leonard, *Songs From a Room*
Cream, *Fresh Cream*
————, *Disraeli Gears*
Creedence Clearwater Revival, *Bayou Country*
Derek and the Dominos, *Layla and other Assorted Love Songs*
The Eagles, *Hotel California*
Eno, Brian, *Before and After Science*
Genesis, *The Lamb Lies Down on Broadway*
Green, Al, *Let's Stay Together*
Hendrix, Jimi, *Are You Experienced?*
————, *Axis: Bold as Love*
————, *Electric Ladyland*
King, Carole, *Tapestry*
King Crimson, *In the Court of the Crimson King*
Led Zeppelin, *Led Zeppelin*
————, *Led Zeppelin II*
Mayall, John, and the Bluesbreakers, *Turning Point*
MC5, *Kick Out the Jams*
Mitchell, Joni, *Court and Spark*
Morrison, Van, *Moondance*
New York Dolls, *Too Much Too Soon*
Newman, Randy, *12 Songs*
Pink Floyd, *The Dark Side of the Moon*
————, *Wish You Were Here*
Ramones, *Ramones*
Reed, Lou, *Transformer*
The Rolling Stones, *Exile on Main Street*
————, *Sticky Fingers*
Roxy Music, *Avalon*
Sly and the Family Stone, *Stand*
Soft Machine, *Third*
Springfield, Dusty, *Dusty in Memphis*
The Stooges, *The Stooges*
The Who, *Tommy*
————, *Who's Next*
Wonder, Stevie, *Talking Book*
Woodstock
Wyatt, Robert, *Rock Bottom*
Young, Neil, *After the Gold Rush*

CHAPTER 6

The B-52s, *The B-52s*
Black Flag, *Damaged*
Blondie, *Parallel Lines*
The Clash, *The Clash*
————, *Sandinista!*
Costello, Elvis, *My Aim is True*
————, *This Year's Model*
The Cramps, *Songs the Lord Taught Us*
Culture Club, *Colour By Numbers*
The Cure, *Pornography*
Dead Kennedys, *Fresh Fruit for Rotting Vegetables*
De La Soul, *Three Feet High and Rising*

Dire Straits, *Brothers in Arms*
Eurythmics, *Sweet Dreams (Are Made of This)*
Fleetwood Mac, *Rumours*
Funkadelic, *One Nation Under a Groove*
Guns 'n' Roses, *Appetite for Destruction*
Harvey, P. J., *Rid of Me*
Hell, Richard, and the Voidoids, *Blank Generation*
Jackson, Joe, *Look Sharp!*
Jackson, Michael, *Off the Wall*
————, *Thriller*
The Jam, *All Mod Cons*
John, Elton, *The Very Best of Elton John*
Joy Division, *Unknown Pleasures*
King Sunny Ade, *Juju Music*
Kuti, Fela Anikulapo, *Black President*
Ladysmith Black Mambazo, *Shaka Zulu*
LL Cool J, *14 Shots to the Dome*
Lynyrd Skynyrd, *Street Survivors*
Madonna, *Like a Virgin*
Marley, Bob, *Babylon by Bus*
————, *Burnin'*
Metallica, *...And Justice for All*
Motörhead, *No Sleep Till Hammersmith*
Nirvana, *Nevermind*
O'Connor, Sinéad, *I Do Not Want What I Haven't Got*
Parker, Graham, *Howlin' Wind*
Pearl Jam, *Ten*
Pere Ubu, *Cloudland*
The Police, *Reggatta de Blanc*
The Pretenders, *The Pretenders*
Prince, *Purple Rain*
Public Enemy, *It Takes a Nation of Millions to Hold Us Back*
Public Image Ltd, *Second Edition*
Queen Latifah, *All Hail the Queen*
The Ramones, *Ramones Leave Home*
The Red Hot Chili Peppers, *Blood Sugar Sex Magik*
REM, *The Best of REM*
————, *Lifes Rich Pageant*
The Rolling Stones, *Some Girls*
Run-D.M.C., *Raising Hell*
The Sex Pistols, *Never Mind the Bollocks Here's the Sex Pistols*
Simon, Paul, *Graceland*
Smith, Patti, *Horses*
Sonic Youth, *Daydream Nation*
Springsteen, Bruce, *Born to Run*
————, *The River*
Stewart, Rod, *Every Picture Tells a Story*
Stiff Little Fingers, *Inflammable Material*
Talking Heads, *Remain in Light*
Television, *Marquee Moon*
Thompson, Richard and Linda, *I Want to See the Lights*
Turner, Tina, *Private Dancer*
U2, *Achtung Baby*
————, *The Joshua Tree*
Waits, Tom, *Rain Dogs*
Winwood, Steve, *Back in the Highlife*
Young, Neil, *Rust Never Sleeps*

FILMOGRAPHY

American Graffiti, dir. George Lucas, 1973

The Decline of Western Civilization, dir. Penelope Spheeris, 1981

The Decline of Western Civilization Part II: The Metal Years, dir. Penelope Spheeris, 1988

Don't Look Back, dir. D. A. Pennebaker, with Bob Dylan, 1967

Gimme Shelter, dir. the Maysles brothers, with the Rolling Stones, 1970

The Girl Can't Help It, dir. Frank Tashlin, with Fats Domino, the Platters and Little Richard, 1956

A Hard Day's Night, dir. Richard Lester, with the Beatles, 1964

The Harder They Come, dir. Perry Henzell, with Jimmy Cliff, 1973

Help!, dir. Richard Lester, with the Beatles, 1965

The Kids Are Alright, dir. Jeff Stein, with the Who, 1979

King Creole, dir. Michael Curtiz, with Elvis Presley, 1958

The Last Waltz, dir. Martin Scorsese, with the Band, 1978

Monterey Pop, dir. Albert Maysles, D. A. Pennebaker, and others, with Jimi Hendrix, Otis Redding, Janis Joplin and others, 1969

Rude Boy, dir. Jack Hazan and David Mingay, with the Clash, 1980

Sid and Nancy, dir. Alex Cox, 1986

The T.A.M.I. Show, dir. Steve Binder, with the Rolling Stones, Chuck Berry, James Brown and others, 1965

This is Spinal Tap, dir. Rob Reiner, 1984

Tommy, dir. Ken Russell, music by the Who, 1975

Woodstock, dir. Michael Wadleigh, with Jimi Hendrix, Joe Cocker, Country Joe and the Fish, and others, 1970

Yellow Submarine, dir. George Dunning, with the Beatles, 1968

FURTHER READING

Bane, Michael, *White Boy Singin' the Blues: The Black Roots of White Rock*, 1982

Bangs, Lester, *Psychotic Reactions and Carburetor Dung*, 1987

Charles, Ray, and David Ritz, *Brother Ray: Ray Charles' Own Story*, 1979

Christgau, Robert, *Rock Albums of the '70s: Christgau's Guide*, 1979

DeCurtis, Anthony, and James Henke, eds., *The Rolling Stone Illustrated History of Rock & Roll*, 1992

Escott, Colin, *Good Rockin' Tonight: Sun Records and the Birth of Rock 'n' Roll*, 1991

Friedman, Myra, *Buried Alive: The Biography of Janis Joplin*, 1992

Frith, Simon, *Sound Effects: Youth, Leisure and the Politics of Rock*, 1983

Gillett, Charlie, *The Sound of the City: The Rise of Rock and Roll*, 1983

Guralnick, Peter, *Feel Like Going Home: Portraits in Blues and Rock 'n' Roll*, 1992

———, *Lost Highway: Journeys and Arrivals of American Musicians*, 1991

———, *Sweet Soul Music: Rhythm and Blues and the Southern Dream of Freedom*, 1986

Hebdige, Dick, *Subculture: The Meaning of Style*, 1979

Heylin, Clinton, ed., *The Penguin Book of Rock 'n' Roll Writing*, 1992

Hopkins, Jerry, *Elvis: The Final Years: A Biography*, 1981

———, and Daniel Sugerman, *No One Here Gets Out Alive*, 1982

Marcus, Greil, *Mystery Train*, 1991

Marsh, Dave, *Springsteen : Born to Run*, 1981

Murray, Charles Shaar, *Crosstown Traffic: Jimi Hendrix and Post-War Pop*, 1991

Nite, Norm, *Rock On: The Illustrated Encyclopedia of Rock 'n' Roll*, 1984

Norman, Philip, *The Stones*, 1984

Rolling Stone Press, *The Ballad of John and Yoko*, 1982

———, *The Rolling Stone Encyclopedia of Rock & Roll*, Pareles, Jon, and Patricia Romanowski, eds., 1983

Savage, Jon, *England's Dreaming: Sex Pistols and Punk Rock*, 1991

Shelton, Robert, *No Direction Home: The Life and Music of Bob Dylan*, 1987

Simpson Jeff, ed., *Radio 1s Classic Interviews: 25 Rock Greats in Their Own Words*, 1992

Stern, Jane, and Michael Stern, *Elvis' World*, 1991

Szatmary, David P., *Rockin' in Time: A Social History of Rock and Roll*, 1991

Thomson, Elizabeth, and David Gutman, *The Lennon Companion: Twenty-Five Years of Comment*, 1987

Tosches, Nick, *Hellfire: The Jerry Lee Lewis Story*, 1982

Ward, Ed, et al., *Rock of Ages: The Rolling Stone History of Rock & Roll*, 1986

Wenner, Jann, *Lennon Remembers: The Rolling Stone Interviews*, 1973

Whitcomb, Ian, *After the Ball: Pop Music from Rag to Rock*, 1974

White, Timothy, *Rock Lives: Profiles and Interviews*, 1990

Zappa, Frank, *The Real Frank Zappa Book*, 1990

LIST OF ILLUSTRATIONS

The following abbreviations have been used: *a* above; *b* below; *c* centre; *l* left; *r* right.

COVER

Front Jimi Hendrix at the Olympia Club in Paris. Photograph by Jean-Louis Rancurel and B Lampard, 1967. Background: Jukebox. Photograph by M. Anderson, 1960
Spine Gibson guitar
Back Detail from the Sex Pistols' *God Save the Queen* 45 rpm record cover. Virgin Records

OPENING

1 and *2* Detail from *Rock and Roll Party* record cover
3 and *4–5* Detail from lobby card for the movie *Don't Knock the Rock,* with Bill Haley and His Comets. Columbia Pictures, 1957
6–7 Detail from lobby card for the movie *Rock, Rock, Rock,* with Alan Freed. DCA, 1956
8–9 Detail from lobby card for movie *Don't Knock the Rock,* with Bill Haley and His Comets. Columbia Pictures, 1957
11 Detail from the Cramps' *Songs the Lord Taught Us* record cover. I.R.S., 1980

CHAPTER 1

12 Detail from Bill Haley's *Rockin' the Joint!* record cover. Vogue Records, 1956
13 Photograph by Bruce Davidson, 1959
14l James Dean. Photograph by Delange, 1955
14br Levi Strauss & Co. blue jeans label
14–5 Marlon Brando, in a still from the film *The Wild One,* directed by Laslo Benedek, 1954
15 Neal Cassady (left) and Jack Kerouac (right). Photograph, 1954. University of Massachusetts, Lowell
16–7a Teenagers. Photograph by Bruce Davidson, 1959
17b Ray Charles. Photograph, July 1961
18a Detail from concert poster for Fats Domino and His Orchestra, 1957
18c Detail from a 'rhythm and blues' postcard, 1955
18b Fats Domino and His Orchestra postcard, 1956
19b Johnnie Ray in a recording studio at Columbia Records. Photograph by Dennis Stock, 1950
20 Concert poster for Elvis Presley. Florida Theater, Jacksonville, Florida, 1956
21a Elvis Presley's *I Wish You a Merry Christmas* record cover. BMG-RCA, 1984

21b Elvis Presley, from *Rock 'n' Roll Jamboree* (magazine). 1956
22–3 Elvis Presley performing at a concert in 1956. Photographs from *Elvis Presley, Tutti Frutti ou l'Erection des Coeurs: Photographies des Années de Gloire du Roi du Rock 'n' Roll, 1954–1960.* Published by Editions Schirmer-Mosel. Paris-Munich
24–5 Poster for Elvis Presley's movie *Loving You.* Paramount, 1957
26l Teenagers (detail). Photograph by Erich Hartmann, 1960
26–7a A church in Savannah, Georgia. Photograph by Stanley Greene, 1991
26–7c Poster for a religious concert. Oakland, California, 1958
26–7b Detail from Little Richard's *Little Richard* record cover. Camden-RCA, 1956
27r Teenagers (detail). Photograph by Erich Hartmann, 1960
28a Detail from a poster for the movie *Don't Knock the Rock,* with Bill Haley and His Comets. Columbia Pictures, 1957
28b Germany 1960. Photograph by René Burri, 1960
29 Detail from poster for the movie *Don't Knock the Rock,* with Bill Haley and His Comets. Columbia Pictures, 1957
30al *Essential Elvis Presley* record cover. RCA, 1988
30ar Advertisement for a scooter. Eclair Mondial, 1950
30b Eddie Cochran. Photograph, 1959. Jean-Louis Rancurel collection
31a Buddy Holly's *The Nashville Sessions* record cover. MCA, 1957
31b Gene Vincent and His Blue Caps. Photograph, 1960. Pathe Marconi-EMI

CHAPTER 2

32 American teenagers. Photograph by Dennis Stock, 1960
33 Jukebox. Photograph by M. Anderson, 1960
34–5 American teenagers. Photograph by Henri Cartier-Bresson, 1960
35 Detail from Chuck Berry's *New Juke Box Hits* record cover. Chess, 1961
36a and *b* Rock festival at the Palais des Sports in Paris. Photograph by Jean-Louis Rancurel, 1961
37a German teenagers. Photograph by Ian Berry, c. 1960
37b Detail from a Platters album cover. Mercury Polygram, 1957
38a Detail from *Let's Go Dancing to Rock and Roll* record cover. 1957

CHAPTER 6

DOCUMENTS

INDEX

ACKNOWLEDGMENTS

The publisher would like to thank Neil Spencer for his immeasurable help in producing this book.

PHOTO CREDITS

TEXT CREDITS

Alain Dister,
writer and photographer,
was born in Lyons, France, in 1941.
His written work has always focused on
rock and roll, and he is the author of
many books and articles on the subject.
His photographs (which span a variety of themes)
have been exhibited in museums and galleries
around the world, and he has produced a number of
music shows for French television.

For Elise and Marie-Hélène

© Gallimard 1992

English translation © Thames and Hudson Ltd., London,
and Harry N. Abrams, Inc., New York, 1993

Translated by Toula Ballas

British Library Cataloguing-in-Publication Data

A catalogue record for this book is available from
the British Library

ISBN 0–500–30033–X

Printed and bound in Italy
by Editoriale Libraria, Trieste